The English New Testament

The
English New Testament

from Tyndale to the
Revised Standard Version

Luther A. Weigle

GREENWOOD PRESS, PUBLISHERS
NEW YORK

Preface

∘◇∘

THIS account of some of the difficulties involved in the effort to translate the New Testament into English—from Tyndale's creative work in the early sixteenth century through the successive revisions which in time gave us the versions of 1611, 1881, 1901, and 1946—is based on a series of Cole lectures at Vanderbilt University. Let me record my appreciation of the appointment as Cole lecturer, and my gratitude for the gracious hospitality of Vanderbilt and Nashville friends, especially of Dean John K. Benton of the School of Religion. I am grateful, too, to the good audiences that came night after night and encouraged me to think that people generally are interested after all in the New Testament and in the problem of what English version to use in public worship and in private study and devotions.

Those who have read the *Introduction to the Revised Standard Version of the New Testament* will note that some of the material which Professor Clarence Tucker Craig and I presented in our chapters in that booklet is repeated here. They will recognize the necessity for some repetition, I hope, and perhaps be the more interested in the large bulk of different material, especially the historical background, which the booklet did not attempt to discuss. It is an absorbing and involved story—and one particularly significant in our time for all who believe in the abiding value of the New Testament.

LUTHER A. WEIGLE

Contents

○○○

7

○-○

The English Bible to 1611

THE language of English translations of the Bible was a major problem of the sixteenth and early seventeenth centuries; and today, more than three hundred years later, it has again become a problem. The problem is how to secure a clear, accurate English version of the Scriptures, which can be understood by the people who read it and hear it read, and which will also be acceptable for use in public worship. The study of how this problem was met and solved in another day may be of help in judging how wisely Bible scholars and Christian ministers are dealing with it in our own day.

To keep the discussion within manageable bounds we shall limit it to the New Testament, and to the authorized versions of the New Testament in English—particularly to the King James Version of 1611 (often referred to as the Authorized Version, especially in England), and its three revisions: the English Revised Version of 1881, the American Standard Version of 1901, and the Revised Standard Version of 1946. Since the discussion is concerned with the English of the New Testament, the problems of the Greek text, Greek vocabulary, and Greek grammar dealt with in more technical works will be referred to only when they are directly related to the present study.

The present situation is depicted in a statement made by the Church of Scotland in 1946:

9

We are fully appreciative of the superb literary qualities of the Authorised Version, its majestic style, its noble cadences and the many excellences which have given it its unique place in our literature and endeared it to generations of Christians in the English-speaking world. But we are compelled to recognise that the Authorised Version is becoming unable to fulfill the function it was created to serve, because the language in which it is written is not the language our people speak, or readily understand, today. . . . Many words and phrases which were current coin in 1611 have fallen out of circulation; many words have changed their meanings, some have appreciated in value, others have depreciated, some have acquired a broader meaning, others a narrower; the general manner of using the language, the style, and even the syntax have changed. The consequence is that to those of our people, especially of the younger generation, who have not had more than an elementary schooling in language and literature, there is a great deal in the Authorised Version which is simply incomprehensible. . . . There is the further danger that even where the language of the Bible is intelligible, the archaic flavour may well give the impression that the message of the Bible itself belongs to a bygone age and has no relevance to the world of the twentieth century.

In view of this situation, the Church of Scotland has proposed to the Church of England and the other churches of Great Britain that they unite in authorizing the making of "a new translation, not a revision of the Authorised Version or of the Revised Version, having as its object to render the original into contemporary English, and avoiding all archaic words and forms of expression."

The churches of the United States and Canada took action earlier, and along a somewhat different line. In 1929 the International Council of Religious Education, in which the educational boards of forty of the major Protestant denominations of these two countries are associated, appointed a committee of scholars to study the situation; and in 1937 it authorized this committee to proceed with a revision of the American Standard Version. The act of authorization stated that the revision should "embody the best results of modern scholarship as to the meaning of the Scriptures, and express this meaning in English diction which is designed for use in public and private worship and preserves those qualities which have given to the King James Version a supreme place in English literature." After nine years of work, the Revised Standard Version of the New Testament was published in 1946; and the committee expects to complete the revision of the Old Testament by 1950.

It may seem strange that the proposal for a wholly new translation should come from Great Britain, and that revision of the authorized versions should be undertaken in America. But this can be understood in the light of the fact that the new translation proposed by the Church of Scotland is intended for use in private study and not for use in the public worship of the church, in which it is assumed that the King James Version will continue to hold its present place; while the Revised Standard Version is designed to be used in public worship. The excellent translations of Moffatt, Weymouth, and Goodspeed are already widely used here in private study, and the American Standard Version of 1901 has been more fully accepted on this side of the Atlantic than the English Revised Version of 1881-85 has been accepted on the other.

Let it be said at once that there is no misunderstanding or competition in this matter between the representatives of Great Britain and those of the United States and Canada. In 1937 conversations with British scholars and churchmen looked toward co-operation in the work of revision, but this proved to be impracticable in the years of war. These conversations were renewed in 1946, and the representatives of the British churches have agreed, even though they have undertaken a translation along the lines proposed by the Church of Scotland, to co-operate with the American committee in the work that remains to be done upon the Revised Standard Version.

A sound translation of the New Testament, like any other translation, depends on four basic requirements:

1. *Accurate text:* a Greek text as close to the original as the scientific study of the ancient manuscripts can take us.

2. *Knowledge of the original language:* accurate knowledge and command of the vocabulary, grammar, and idioms of the Greek in which the books of the New Testament were written.

3. *Knowledge of the language into which the translation is made:* adequate knowledge and command of the vocabulary, grammar, and idioms of English from the time of Wycliffe until today.

4. *Penetration to the spirit of the original text*: as faithful reproduction of the spirit of the original writers of the New Testament as can be gained.

Translation is an art—an art that uses and builds upon the results of the scientific investigation of text, vocabulary, and grammar. Of all characteristics of a sound translation the reproduction of the spirit of the original text is the most difficult to attain. It is as rare and as elusive as is the best in any art. It may be hindered by the temperament, character, and spirit of the translator; or by the refractoriness of the language into which the translation is made; or by the temperament, character and experience of the people for whom the translation is made and the spirit of the age in which they live.

The history of English translations of the Bible is a long and complicated story. It may be read in such standard works as those by Bishop Westcott and Professor John Eadie, or in the recent collection of essays on *The Bible in Its Ancient and English Versions* edited by Principal H. Wheeler Robinson. There is need for us only to recall the outstanding facts and dates, as a basis for the discussion which is to follow.

The first English versions of the entire Bible were the two associated with the work of John Wycliffe, made by translation from the Latin Vulgate between 1380 and 1400. They were copied by hand, and there remain some one hundred and eighty manuscripts, mostly of the second version. The first version is an extremely literal translation of the Vulgate, which closely follows the order of the Latin words; the second version, which has been attributed to John Purvey, is a freer, more natural translation into English.

The first English version of the Scriptures to be made by direct translation from the original Hebrew and Greek, and the first to be printed, was the work of William Tyndale. Part of a quarto edition of his translation of the New Testament was published at Cologne in 1525, and the entire translation of the New Testament was published at Worms in 1526. These were followed by the publication of his translation of the Pentateuch in 1530 and of Jonah in 1531. In 1534 he issued a revision of his translation of Genesis and a revision of his translation of the New Testament. Finally *The New Testament yet once again corrected by William Tyndale* was published in 1535; and this became the basis of all later revisions, and the main source of the authorized versions of the New Testament in English.

Tyndale met bitter opposition. He was accused of willfully perverting the meaning of the Scriptures; and his New

Testaments were ordered to be burned as "untrue translations," intended "for the advancement and setting forth of
Luther's abominable heresies." He was finally betrayed into
the hands of his enemies, and early in October, 1536, was
publicly executed and burned at the stake. His last words
were: "Lord, open the King of England's eyes."

In 1535 there appeared an English translation of the Bible
by Miles Coverdale. This was the first complete Bible to be
printed in English. It was not, like the work of Tyndale, a
firsthand translation from the original languages; it was based
upon the Latin Vulgate and upon the existing translations of
Tyndale into English, of Luther and of Zwingli and his as-
sociates into German, and of Pagninus into Latin.

In 1537 a folio volume was published entitled *The Bible,
which is all the Holy Scriptures, in which are contayned the
Olde and Newe Testaments, truely and purely translated into
Englysh, by Thomas Matthew.* This was a compilation, edited
by John Rogers, of translations by Tyndale and Coverdale.
"Thomas Matthew" was a pseudonym taken by Rogers, who
was a friend of Tyndale and was destined himself to become
the first martyr under Queen Mary. After Tyndale's execu-
tion in 1536, Rogers took Tyndale's manuscript translations,
as yet unpublished, of the books of the Old Testament from
Joshua to Second Chronicles, together with Tyndale's published translations of the Pentateuch, Jonah, and the New
Testament, and published them all in this one volume, which
he completed by adding Coverdale's version of the rest of the
Old Testament and the Apocrypha. At the request of Archbishop Cranmer, Rogers' edition of the Bible, which was
about two thirds the work of Tyndale and one third the work
of Coverdale, was granted the royal license; and it is thus the
first English authorized version. Similar authorization was

given to Coverdale's version in the same year. It is Rogers' Bible, however, which became the foundation of all later English authorized versions, and it is through Rogers' republication that Tyndale's 1535 version of the New Testament had its great influence upon subsequent revisions.

In connection with the authorization of Rogers' edition of the Bible a declaration was drafted, to be read by the curates to the people in all the churches. It is worth quoting, for it expresses the spirit of the efforts toward reform that were being made by Archbishop Cranmer and Thomas Cromwell, who was then vicar-general and vice-regent:

Whereas it hath pleased the king's majesty, our most dread sovereign, and supreme head under God of this Church of England, for a declaration of the great zeal he beareth to the setting forth of God's word, and to the virtuous maintenance of the commonwealth, to permit and command the Bible, being translated into our mother tongue, to be sincerely taught by us the curates, and to be openly laid forth in every parish church: to the intent that all his good subjects, as well by reading thereof, as by hearing the true explanation of the same, may be able to learn their duties to Almighty God and his majesty, and every of us charitably to use other: and then applying themselves to do according to that they shall hear and learn, may both speak and do Christianly; and in all things as it beseemeth Christian men: because his highness very much desireth, that this thing being by him most godly begun and set forward, may of all you be received as is aforesaid; his majesty hath willed and commanded this to be declared unto you, that his grace's pleasure and high commandment is, that in the reading and hearing thereof, first most humbly and reverently using and addressing yourselves unto it, you shall have always in your remembrance and memories, that all things contained in this Book is the undoubted will, law, and commandment of Almighty God, the only and straight means to know the goodness and benefits of God towards us, and the true duty of every Christian man to serve him accordingly. And that therefore reading this Book with such mind and firm faith as is aforesaid, you shall first endeavour yourselves to conform your own livings and conversation to the contents of the same. And so by your good and virtuous example to encourage your wives, children, and servants to live well and Christianly according to the rules thereof.

And if at any time by reading any doubt shall come to any of you touching the sense and meaning of any part thereof, that then, not giving too much to your own minds, fantasies, and opinions; nor having thereof any open reasoning in your open taverns or alehouses and other places, ye shall have recourse to such learned men as be or shall be authorized to preach and declare the same. So that, avoiding all contentions and disputation in such alehouses and other places, unmeet for such conferences, and submitting your opinion to the judgments of such learned men as shall be appointed in this behalf, his grace may well perceive that you use this most high benefit quietly and charitably every one of you, to the edifying of himself, his wife, and family, in all things answering to his highness' good opinion conceived of you, in the advancement of virtue and suppressing of vice; without failing to use such discreet quietness and sober moderation in the premises as is aforesaid; as you tender his grace's pleasure, and intend to avoid his high indignation, and the peril and danger that may ensue to you and every of you for the contrary.

In 1538 Coverdale issued a diglot New Testament, containing in parallel columns the Latin Vulgate and an English translation of the Latin. His purpose was to disarm criticism by showing that an English New Testament could faithfully represent the Latin which was used in the services of the Church, and to aid both priests and people to understand the

New Testament by facilitating comparison of the Latin and English versions.

In 1539 Richard Taverner, a layman and lawyer, a member of the staff of Thomas Cromwell, and clerk of the signet to the king, published a revision of Matthew's (Rogers') Bible, one edition of which was issued in parts in order that poorer people who could not afford to purchase the whole Bible might buy one or more parts. He was a good Greek scholar, and made some changes that have been kept in later versions. In a formal dedication to the king he wrote:

This one thing I dare well affirm, that amongst all your majesty's deservings . . . your highness never did thing more acceptable unto God, more profitable to the advancement of true Christianity, more unpleasant to the enemies of the same, and also to your grace's enemies, than when your majesty licensed and willed the most sacred Bible containing the unspotted and lively Word of God to be in the English tongue set forth to your highness' subjects. . . . Forasmuch as the printers hereof were very desirous to have the Bible come forth as faultless, and emendably as the shortness of time for the recognizing of the same would require, they desired me, for default of a better learned, diligently to overlook and peruse the whole copy; and in any case I should find any notable default that needed correction, to amend the same, according to the true exemplars, which thing according to my talent I have gladly done.

He went on to describe the "great difficulty so absolutely to translate the Holy Bible that it be faultless," and added that he "feared it could scarce be done of one or two persons, but rather required both a deeper conferring of learned wits together, and also a juster time and longer leisure."

Neither of the versions that had received the royal license in 1537 was satisfactory. Coverdale's was easy to read and happily phrased, but it had been made from other translations and was in many instances too far from the original text. Matthew's was largely the work of Tyndale; it kept his bitterly opposed prologue to the epistle to the Romans, and some of its marginal notes were no less controversial.

It was in the national interest, therefore, that another version be secured, more accurate than Coverdale's and without the polemical features of Matthew's. Early in 1538 Thomas Cromwell determined that such a version should be prepared; that it should be printed in Paris, where better paper and superior craftsmanship were to be had; and that he would advance funds to meet the cost of preparation and printing. He assigned the task to Coverdale, who had already published two translations, as we have seen. The choice of Coverdale was justified not only by his experience, but by his character. In dedications of his prior versions Coverdale had written: "No less do I esteem it my duty to amend other men's faults, than if they were my own"; and again: "I am always willing and ready to do my best as well in one translation as in another." A cynical construction is sometimes put upon these sentences, and Coverdale is patronizingly described as acquiescent, complaisant, and pliable. But it is only in a good sense that these terms may justly be applied to him. There is no evidence whatever that Cromwell influenced his choice of words and construction of sentences in the revision which he now undertook. Coverdale simply accepted a task which he saw to be in the public interest, and which could be done without compromise of either scholarship or conscience. He was characterized by unselfishness and objectivity of mind rather than by any undue pliability.

The result of his work was the Great Bible, as it came to be called, which was published in 1539. It is a revision of Matthew's Bible—which means, in other words, that it is Cover-dale's revision of Tyndale's translation of the New Testament and the Old Testament as far as the end of Second Chronicles, and Coverdale's revision of his own translation of the Old Testament from Ezra to Malachi and the Apocrypha. It contains no notes, and Coverdale's short preface indicates that those which he had planned, and for which he had inserted reference marks in the text, were omitted in the public interest.

The market was ready for the Great Bible, for Cromwell, as vicar-general, had issued injunctions to the clergy in September of the previous year which including the following:

Item, that ye shall provide on this side the feast of ———— next coming, one book of the whole Bible in the largest volume in English, and the same set up in some convenient place within the said church that ye have cure of, whereat your parishioners may most commodiously resort to the same and read it; the charges of which book shall be ratably borne between the parson and the parishioners aforesaid, that is to say, the one half by you, and the other half by them.

A second edition of the Great Bible, further revised by Coverdale, was published in 1540, with a persuasive preface by Archbishop Cranmer. On its title page appeared for the first time the phrase: "This is the Bible appointed to the use of the churches." Two more editions were published in 1540, and three in 1541.

In the full sense of the term the Great Bible was authorized, and a copy was ordered to be placed in every church. It is thus often accounted the first authorized version, ignoring the fact that royal license had been given to Matthew's Bible and

Coverdale's Bible in 1537. Some of the bishops who were out of sympathy with Cranmer's measures of reform sought to keep it from publication.

Being demanded by the king what was their judgment of the translation, they answered that there was many faults therein. "Well," said the king, "but are there any heresies maintained thereby?" They answered, there were no heresies they could find maintained thereby. "If there be no heresies," said the king, "then, in God's name, let it go abroad among our people."

Under Queen Mary, who sought to bring England back to obedience to the Pope, no more English Bibles were printed, and the use of the English Bible in the churches was discontinued. Among the nearly three hundred persons who were burned at the stake were John Rogers and Archbishop Cranmer. Some eight hundred English citizens sought refuge on the Continent, and a group of these at Geneva undertook the revision of the English Bible. A version of the New Testament, edited by William Whittingham, was published in 1557; and the Geneva version of the entire Bible, including a revision of Whittingham's New Testament, appeared in April, 1560. In a number of respects it marks a new departure. It was set in Roman type instead of the old blackface; and it was a quarto, easy to handle, instead of a heavy, unwieldy folio. Its pages measured 9 by 6¼ inches, whereas the page of the Great Bible was 15 by 9 inches. It facilitated reference to particular passages by introducing the division into chapters and verses which scholars and publishers were beginning to employ. Its marginal notes were fresh and vigorous, and furnished a sort of running commentary, distinctly evangelical in character, but not as polemical as some of Tyndale's notes.

The Geneva Bible was never authorized, but it did not need to be. It became at once the people's book, the household Bible of the English-speaking nations; and it held this place for three quarters of a century. It was Shakespeare's Bible; and it was the Bible of the Puritans who settled New England. Between 1560 and 1644 at least 140 editions of the Geneva Bible or New Testament were printed; and it lasted longer in competition with the King James Version than any other English version.

This popularity was justified by its merit as a translation. Next to Tyndale the Geneva Bible contributed most to the shaping of the King James Version. Its English style, says Professor Eadie, "made before the birth of Shakespeare, is clear, crisp, and vigorous—the honest and hearty speech of men who felt that their mother tongue needed not to be helped with elaborate combinations, nor studded with foreign terms, for its power lay in its simplicity, and its grandeur in its more familiar idioms."

Soon after her accession Queen Elizabeth renewed the injunction that a copy of "the whole Bible of the largest volume in English" be placed in every church, and encouraged its reading. Because they lacked a sufficient number of copies of the Great Bible, and because many of these were "faultily printed," Archbishop Parker revived a proposal that had been made in Cranmer's day, but had then come to nothing—the proposal that the bishops themselves make a new revision of the English Bible. Parker might have given another reason which he did not state—that the growing popularity of the Geneva Bible made necessary the preparation of a new authorized version, lest Puritanism and Nonconformity prevail.

He allotted the various books of the Bible among twelve bishops and four lesser ecclesiastical officials, with instructions to follow the Great Bible "and not to recede from it but where it varieth manifestly from the Hebrew and Greek original," to make use of the newer Latin versions of the Old Testament, to refrain from bitter or controversial notes, to mark sections not edifying for public reading, and to substitute more convenient terms and phrases for all such words as tend "to any offence of lightness or obscenity."

The resulting version, known as the Bishops' Bible, was published as a beautiful and stately folio, in 1568. It was authorized by Convocation, and its possession enjoined upon the churches "so far as it could conveniently be done." In 1572 another edition was published, with considerable revision of the New Testament. It is this revised edition of 1572, as reprinted in 1602, that became the basis of the revision under King James. The Bishops' Bible gradually displaced the Great Bible, which was not reprinted after 1569; but in popular use the Geneva Bible retained its pre-eminent position.

In 1582, as part of a plan to win England back to the Papacy, an English translation of the New Testament was published at Rheims, made from the Latin Vulgate by Roman Catholic scholars, the larger part of the work being done by Gregory Martin, who had been trained as a scholar at Oxford University. A similar translation of the Old Testament, in which also Martin had taken the lead, was not published until 1609, at Douai. The distinctive characteristic of the Rhemish version of the New Testament is the closeness with which it adheres to the Latin, which brought about in some cases an enrichment of its vocabulary, and in other cases reduced it to awkwardness and even incomprehensibility. For example, in Phil. 2.7, where Tyndale, the Great Bible, the Geneva Bible, and the Bishops' Bible had said of Christ Jesus, "he made himself of no reputation," the Rhemish version has, "he exinanited himself." Again, where these prior versions had, in Heb. 13.16, "to do good and to distribute forget not, for with such sacrifices God is pleased," the Rhemish version reads, "Beneficence and communication do not forget, for with such hostes God is promerited."

Queen Elizabeth died in 1603, and King James VI of Scotland succeeded her, becoming King James I of England. Because of his Presbyterian upbringing the Puritans cherished high hopes, and Archbishop Whitgift, their chief enemy, expressed foreboding that "a Scottish mist" was descending upon the land. They presented a petition stating the points at which they desired relief from the "burden of human rites and ceremonies," and James called a conference "for hearing and for the determining things pretended to be amiss in the church." It met at Hampton Court Palace on January 14, 16, and 18, 1604; and the four Puritan ministers who had been summoned to attend found themselves confronted by nine bishops, seven deans and archdeacons, and five ecclesiastical lawyers—to say nothing of the king himself. It is true that James spoke for five hours on the corruptions of the church, in such terms that Bishop Andrewes is reported to have said that "on that day his majesty did wonderfully play the Puritan." But it soon became clear that he was only having "revel with the Puritans" and in the end he "peppered them soundly"—to quote two phrases which James himself used in a letter describing the conference. When he roundly declared, "I will make them conform themselves, or I will harry them out of the land, or do worse," Whitgift, archbishop of

Canterbury, in grateful awe, said that he spoke by "the special assistance of God's spirit," and Bancroft, bishop of London, sank on his knees, giving thanks to God for "the singular mercy of such a king, as since Christ the like had not been seen."

The leader of the four Puritans was Dr. John Reynolds, president of Corpus Christi College, Oxford, formerly dean of Lincoln, one of the most learned men of his time, who was alternately snubbed, upbraided, and ridiculed by the king. The only thing that Reynolds secured was the adoption of what seems to have been a chance suggestion which he made in the course of debate. "He moved his Majesty," says the old account, "that there might be a new translation of the Bible because those which were allowed in the reign of King Henry the eighth and Edward the sixth were corrupt and not answerable to the truth of the original." No one opposed the motion, though the bishop of London somewhat sourly remarked that "if every man's humor should be followed, there would be no end of translating." King James welcomed the proposal, and made some supercilious comments on the defects of all translations of the Bible into English that had hitherto been made, especially mentioning the Geneva Bible as "worst of all." He is further reported as saying that he was acquainted with the notes of the Geneva Bible because a copy had been given him by an English lady—which is sheer nonsense! The Geneva Bible is the version on which he had been brought up, and the one which he had quoted in his own writings. Either he has been misreported, or, as Professor Eadie puts it, "his virtual disclaimer of all knowledge up to a late period of the Genevan notes and version was simply a bold unblushing falsehood, a clumsy attempt to sever himself from his earlier Scottish beliefs and usages that he might win favour with his English churchmen."

Be that as it may, and whether from highly worthy or less worthy motives, King James ordained, as set forth in an account corrected with his own hand and dated February 10, 1604: "That a translation be made of the whole Bible, as consonant as can be to the original Hebrew and Greek; and this to be set out and printed without any marginal notes, and only to be used in all churches of England in time of divine service."

The king charged all the bishops to aid in meeting the expense of the work, and in securing suggestions from all competent scholars within their dioceses. He appointed fifty-four men as translators, forty-seven of whom are named in the records that have come down to us. Of these, forty are known as men of proved scholarship, while of seven we know comparatively little. They worked in six companies, to each of which was assigned a section of the Bible. Two of these companies met at Westminster, two at Oxford, and two at Cambridge.

The nature of the undertaking was carefully defined in a list of "The Rules to be observed in the Translation of the Bible," of which the following are of especial importance:

1. The ordinary Bible read in the Church, commonly called the *Bishops Bible,* to be followed, and as little altered as the truth of the original will permit.

3. The old Ecclesiastical Words to be kept, viz. the Word *Church* not to be translated *Congregation* etc.

6. No marginal notes at all to be affixed, but only for the explanation of the *Hebrew* or *Greek* Words, which cannot without some circumlocution, so briefly and fitly be express'd in the Text.

14. These translations to be used when they agree better

with the Text than the Bishops Bible: Tindall's, Matthews, Coverdale's, Whitchurch's, Geneva.

It was provided that each company would consider the work of each other company, and that differences would be resolved by correspondence if possible, and if not, be referred to the general meeting at the end. This was a meeting at London of a committee of six, made up of two representatives from the companies at each of the three centers, which devoted nine months to bringing together and finally editing the work. It was then seen through the press by Dr. Thomas Bilson, bishop of Winchester, and Dr. Myles Smith, of Oxford University; and Smith wrote an extended and informative preface, entitled "The Translators to the Reader."

This version of the Bible, with a fulsome dedication to King James, was published in 1611, under the title: *The Holy Bible, Conteyning the Old Testament and the New. Newly Translated out of the Originall tongues: and with the former translations, diligently compared and revised by his Majesty's Speciall Commandment. Appointed to be read in Churches. Imprinted at London by Robert Barker, Printer to the King's Most Excellent Majesty. Anno Dom. 1611.*

The printing of the Bishops' Bible had ceased when the new version was undertaken; and the King James Bible at once took its place as the authorized version for use in the churches. The Geneva Bible, however, continued to be printed until 1644, and was widely used, not only for private reading, but in the writings and sermons even of some of the bishops.

It is a curious fact that no evidence has yet been found that the King James Version was ever authorized in the sense of being publicly sanctioned by Convocation or by Parliament or by the Privy Council or by the King. But it did not need that. Bishop Westcott, writing in 1868, said:

From the middle of the seventeenth century, the King's Bible has been the acknowledged Bible of the English-speaking nations throughout the world simply because it is the best. A revision which embodied the ripe fruits of nearly a century of labour, and appealed to the religious instinct of a great Christian people, gained by its own internal character a vital authority which could never have been secured by any edict of sovereign rulers.

II

oooooooooooooooooooooooooooooooooooooooooooooo

The Church and the English
Vernacular

THE movement for a vernacular English Bible, from
Tyndale to the King James Version, was part of the general
movement that took the Church of England from the control
of the Papacy. The Bible of the Roman church was the
Latin Vulgate, and the language of its worship was Latin.
Generally speaking the Roman Catholics in sixteenth-century
England and those of the Church of England who were
anxious to retain as much as possible of Catholic faith and
practice either opposed the use of the Bible in the English
vernacular or viewed it with misgiving; while those in
sympathy with the Protestant reformers espoused and
furthered it.

The attitude of the medieval Church toward vernacular
translations from the Bible was one of "toleration in principle
and distrust in practice," says Margaret Deanesley at the close
of her thorough and competent study of the subject. Translations were permitted for missionary purposes, to aid in the
conversion of non-Christian peoples; and among people
already professing the Christian faith, translations of parts of
the Bible were permitted as aids to devotion and in manuals
of religious instruction. Paraphrases of Scripture were favored
rather than exact translations, however; and there was no

objection to biblical stories, glosses, and homilies in the vernacular since these could not be quoted as having the authority of Scripture itself.

The principle that underlay the attitude of the medieval Church toward the use of the vernacular is expressed in a letter written by Pope Gregory VII in 1079 to Vratislaus, king of Bohemia, who had asked permission for his monks to recite the divine office in the Slavonic language:

Since your excellency has asked that we would allow the divine office to be said among you in Slavonic, know that we can by no means favourably answer this your petition. For it is clear to those who reflect often upon it, that not without reason has it pleased Almighty God that holy scripture should be a secret in certain places, lest, if it were plainly apparent to all men, perchance it would be little esteemed and be subject to disrespect; or it might be falsely understood by those of mediocre learning, and lead to error. Nor does it avail as an excuse that certain religious men have patiently suffered the simple folk who asked for it, or have sent them away uncorrected; since the primitive Church allowed many things to pass unheeded, which, after Christianity had grown stronger, and when religion was increasing, were corrected by subtle examination. Wherefore we forbid what you have so imprudently demanded of the authority of S. Peter, and we command you to resist this vain rashness with all your might, to the honour of Almighty God.

As the medieval Church grew more corrupt, and men began to criticize it and to base their criticism upon the Scriptures, the attitude of the Church toward vernacular translations hardened. It was held that the vernacular is too rude to express the great concepts of Christian faith, and that the attempt to translate these from the Latin into the language of the people introduces erroneous connotations, breeds pride of opinion, and leads to sectarian contentions and to heresy. The Church has the truth, it was maintained; and without its guidance private judgment falls into individualism and error. There is always need, therefore, of the Church's authoritative interpretation of the Scriptures. And it is not only unnecessary for the people to understand the language of the Church's worship; it is better that they should not. For worship in an unknown or archaic tongue heightens the mystery of divine grace and awakens reverence; it conveys a sense, moreover, of the oneness and changelessness of Catholic faith and practice.

Pope Innocent III wrote to the people of Metz in 1199:

The secret mysteries of the faith ought not to be explained to all men in all places, since they cannot be everywhere understood by all men; but only to those who can conceive them with a faithful mind, for what says the apostle to simple people? *Even as babes in Christ I have fed you with milk and not with meat.* . . . For such is the depth of divine scripture, that not only the simple and illiterate, but even the prudent and learned, are not fully sufficient to try to understand it. *For many seek and fail in their search,* whence it was of old rightly written in the divine law, that *the beast which touched the mount should be stoned:* lest, apparently, any simple and unlearned person should presume to attain to the sublimity of holy scripture. . . . *Seek not out the things that are above thee.* For what says the apostle? *Not to think more highly than one ought to think, but to think soberly.*

From the Norman Conquest in 1066 until the time of Wycliffe the written vernacular of England was French. Not until 1362 was Parliament opened in English, and pleading in English allowed in the courts of law. Wycliffe shares with Chaucer the glory of creative service to English literature. If Chaucer is to be regarded as the father of English poetry, Wycliffe is the father of English prose. And Wycliffe was the first to conceive the idea of a translation of the entire Bible into English for the use of all the people.

A contemporary chronicler, the continuator of Henry Knighton's work, wrote thus concerning Wycliffe:

Christ gave His Gospel to the clergy and learned of the Church that they might give it to the laity and weaker persons, according to the exigency of the time and the need of the persons. But this Master John Wyclif translated the Gospel from the Latin into the Anglican language not the angelican. And Wyclif, by thus translating the Bible, made it the property of the masses and common to all and more open to the laity and even to women who were able to read than formerly it had been even to the scholarly and most learned of the clergy. And so the Gospel pearl is thrown before swine and trodden underfoot and that which used to be so dear to both clergy and laity has become a joke and this precious gem of the clergy has been turned into the sport of the laity, so that what used to be the highest gift of the clergy and the learned members of the Church has become common to the laity.

Archbishop Arundel, writing to the Pope in 1412, referred to Wycliffe as "that wretched and pestilent fellow of damnable memory, son of the old serpent, and the very herald and child of anti-christ, . . . who crowned his wickedness by translating the Scriptures into the mother tongue." Under Arundel's leadership the provincial council of Oxford enacted thirteen constitutions dealing with the Lollards, as Wycliffe's followers came to be known. The seventh of these reads:

> Since it is dangerous, as S. Jerome witnesses, to translate the text of holy scripture from one language into another, because in such translations the same meaning is not easily retained in all particulars: even as S. Jerome, although he was inspired. confessed that he had often erred in this matter: therefore we decree and ordain that no one shall in future translate on his own authority any text of holy scripture into the English tongue or into any other tongue, by way of book, booklet, or treatise. Nor shall any man read this kind of book, booklet or treatise, now recently composed in the time of the said John Wycliffe, or later, or any that shall be composed in future, in whole or part, publicly or secretly, under penalty of the greater excommunication, until that translation shall be recognized and approved by the diocesan of the place, or if the matter demand it, by a provincial council.

As a countermove to the Wycliffe translations of the Bible Archbishop Arundel licensed in 1410 an English translation of the *Meditationes Vitae Christi* ascribed to Bonaventura, which was published under the title *The Mirrour of the Blessed Life of Jesu Christ*. In 1431 the Bishop of Bath and Wells forbade the possession of English translations of the Bible; and in 1514 one of the articles of the condemnation of Richard Hun was: "He defendeth the translation of the Bible and the holy scripture into the English tongue, which is prohibited by the laws of our mother, holy Church."

The new attitude toward the English translation of the Scriptures which gradually emerged in the sixteenth century was due to the New Learning fostered by the Renaissance, to the Protestant Reformation on the continent of Europe, and to the incarnation of these two strains of influence in the single-minded devotion and sound scholarship of William Tyndale. It was greatly furthered, moreover, by the development of the new art and business of printing.

Outstanding among the exponents of the New Learning was Erasmus, who wrote his *Enchiridion Militis Christiani* or *Manual of the Christian Knight* in 1502, produced a new Latin version of the New Testament in 1505, and published the first edition of his Greek New Testament in 1516. In the Paraclesis, or exhortation, prefixed to the Greek New Testament Erasmus wrote:

I vehemently dissent from those who are unwilling that the sacred scriptures, translated into the vulgar tongue, should be read by private persons. Christ wishes his mysteries to be published as widely as possible. I wish even all women to read the gospel and the Epistles of Saint Paul, and I wish that they were translated into the tongues of all men. . . . I would to God that the ploughman would sing a text of Scripture at his plough-beam; and the weaver at his loom with this would drive away the tediousness of time. I would the wayfaring man with this pastime would expel the weariness of his journey. And, to be short, I would that all the communication of the Christian should be of the Scripture; for a manner, such are we ourselves, as our daily tales are. . . . We cannot call any man a Platonist, unless he have read the works of Plato. Yet call we them Christian, yea and divines, which never have read the Scriptures of Christ.

There is an echo of these words of Erasmus in Foxe's account of the young Tyndale's reply to his opponent: "If God spare my life, ere many years I will cause a boy that driveth the plough shall know more of the scripture than thou dost." Erasmus was not himself qualified to make a vernacular translation, but his Greek New Testament was used by Luther as the basis for the translation into German, and by Tyndale for the translation into English.

We may distinguish seven issues that were involved in the development of the English Bible in the eighty-five years between the publication of Tyndale's first New Testament in 1526 and the publication of the King James Version in 1611:

1. Shall there be an English translation of the Bible?
2. If so, shall the English Bible be in the hands of the people?
3. Shall the English Bible contain only a translation of the Hebrew, Greek or Latin text, or shall it also have notes, explanatory glosses, and prologues or prefaces to the various books?
4. Shall the English Bible be read, and the English language be used, in the services of the Church?
5. Shall the English Bible retain the old ecclesiastical words?
6. Shall the translation be made from the Latin Vulgate or from the original Hebrew and Greek?
7. Shall it use only native English words of Anglo-Saxon origin or words of Latin derivation?

1. That there should be a printed and published English translation of the Bible admitted of no doubt, once Tyndale's work appeared. Denunciations and prohibitions could not stop it; the buying and burning of thousands of copies simply furnished funds for the printing of more. And people were determined to have it. Bishop Nix in 1530 implored the help of the king, saying that the movement was beyond his power to suppress, and that if it should continue, "I think they shall undo us all." In June of that year the king issued a proclamation condemning Tyndale's books and requiring all who had

copies to surrender them. This proclamation went on to deal
with the basic issue as follows:

And furthermore, for as much as it is come to the hearing of
our said sovereign lord the king, that report is made by divers
and many of his subjects, that as it were to all men not only
expedient, but also necessary, to have in the English tongue
both the New Testament and the Old: and that his highness,
his noble men and prelates were bounden to suffer them so to
have it; His highness hath therefore semblably there upon consulted with the said primates and virtuous, discrete, and well
learned personages in divinity foresaid, and by them all it is
thought, that it is not necessary, the said scripture to be in the
English tongue, and in the hands of the common people; but
that the distribution of the said scripture, and their permitting
or denying thereof, dependeth only upon the discretion of the
superiors, as they shall think it convenient. And that having
respect to the malignity of this present time, with the inclination
of the people to erroneous opinions, the translation of the New
Testament and the Old into the vulgar tongue of English, should
rather be the occasion of continuance or increase of errors among
the said people, than any benefit or commodity toward the
weal of their souls. And that it shall now be more convenient that
the same people have the holy scripture expounded to them,
by preachers in their sermons, according as it hath been of old
time accustomed before this time.

These sentences are immediately followed, however, by a
conditional promise:

All be it if it shall hereafter appear to the king's highness, that
his said people do utterly abandon and forsake all perverse,
erroneous, and seditious opinions, with the New Testament and
the Old, corruptly translated into the English tongue now being

in print: And that the same books and all other books of heresy, as well in the French tongue as in the Dutch tongue, be clearly exterminated and exiled out of this realm of England forever: his highness extendeth to provide, that the holy scripture shall be by great learned and catholic persons, translated into the English tongue, if it shall then seem to his grace convenient so to be.

Hugh Latimer, who was then one of the king's chaplains, reminded him of this promise and asked its fulfillment, in a bold and earnest letter on December 1, 1530. Four years later, in December, 1534, "the bishops, abbots, and priors of the upper house of convocation, or the second synod of the province of Canterbury," petitioned the king "to decree that the holy Scripture shall be translated into the vulgar English tongue by certain upright and learned men to be named by the said most illustrious king and be meted out and delivered to the people for their instruction." They added that he should "command, with a penalty assigned and imposed, that no layman or secular person among his subjects should for the future presume publicly to dispute or in any manner to wrangle concerning the catholic faith, or the articles of the faith, the Holy Scripture or its meaning."

Archbishop Cranmer proposed that a translation be made by the bishops, but the plan failed. Bishop Gardiner, despite his Catholic conservatism, did his share. But Bishop Stokesley was defiant. When asked why he had not returned his portion, he answered:

I marvel what my Lord of Canterbury meaneth, that thus abuseth the people, in giving them liberty to read the Scriptures, which doth nothing else but infect them with heresy. I have bestowed never an hour upon my portion, nor never will; and, therefore, my lord shall have this book again, for I will never be guilty of bringing the common people into error.

Finally the question as to whether or not an English translation of the Bible should exist and be recognized as lawful to possess and read was settled by the royal licensing of Matthew's Bible and Coverdale's Bible in 1537, by Cromwell's Injunctions of 1538, by the authorization of the Great Bible, and by the king's proclamation of May 6, 1541, enforcing the Injunctions, and requiring the possession in every church of "Bibles of the largest and greatest volume."

2. We turn now to the second question: Shall the English Bible be in the hands of the people? Sir Thomas More, whom Bishop Tunstall secured to be the literary opponent of Tyndale, took the position that it is well to have the Bible translated into English, provided it is done by "some good catholic and well learned man, or by divers, dividing the labour among them, and after conferring their several parts together each with other," and provided that their work is approved by the bishops. But he proposed that the English Bible be afforded only a limited and strictly controlled circulation. All copies, in any diocese, should be owned by the bishop, who would at his discretion loan a copy "to such as he perceiveth honest, sad, and virtuous, with a good monition and fatherly counsel to use it reverently with humble heart and lowly mind, rather seeking therein occasion of devotion than of discussion." After the decease of the person to whom it was loaned the book must be "brought again and reverently restored" to the bishop.

So that, as near as may be devised, no man have it but of the ordinary's hand, and by him thought and reputed for such as shall be likely to use it to God's honour and merit of his own soul.

Among whom, if any be proved after to have abused it, then the use thereof to be forboden him, either for ever, or till he be waxen wiser.

In defense of this proposal More used the analogy of medicine and the physician:

It were not unreasonable that the ordinary whom God hath in the diocese appointed for the chief physician to discern between the whole and the sick, and between disease and disease, should after his wisdom and discretion appoint everybody their part, as he should perceive to be good and wholesome for them. And therefore as he should not fail to find many a man to whom he might commit all the whole, so, to say the truth, I can see none harm therein, though he should commit unto some man the gospel of Matthew, Mark or Luke, whom he should yet forbid the gospel of St. John, and suffer some to read the Acts of the Apostles, whom he would not suffer to meddle with the Apocalips. Many were there I think that should take much profit by saint Paules epistle *ad Ephesios,* wherein he giveth good counsel to every kind of people, and yet should find little fruit for their understanding in his epistle *ad Romanos,* containing such high difficulties as very few learned men can very well attain. . . . So that, as I say, though the bishop might unto some layman betake and commit with good advice and instruction the whole Bible to read, yet might he to some man well and with reason restrain the reading of some part, and from some busybody the meddling with any part at all, more than he shall hear in sermons set out and declared unto him; and, in likewise, to take the Bible away from such folk again, as be proved by their blind presumption to abuse the occasion of their profit unto their own hurt and harm. And thus may the bishop order the scripture in our hands with as good reason as the father doeth by his discretion appoint which of his children may for his sadness keep a knife to cut his meat, and which of his wantonness have his knife taken from him for cutting of his fingers.

This proposal was never adopted. Something like it was implied in the 1534 petition of the Convocation of Canterbury, as we have seen; but the fourth of Cromwell's Injunctions of 1538 was:

Item, that ye discourage no man privily or apertly from the reading or hearing of the same Bible, but shall expressly provoke, stir, and exhort every person to read the same, as that which is the very lively word of God, that every Christian man is bound to embrace, believe, and follow, if he look to be saved; admonishing them nevertheless, to avoid all contention, altercation therein, and to use an honest sobriety in the inquisition of the true sense of the same, and refer the explication of obscure places, to men of higher judgment in Scripture.

This was enforced by the king's proclamation in 1541, which expressly stated that access to the Bible was to be afforded to "every of the king's Majesty's loving subjects, minding to read therein." The right of private persons to purchase English Bibles was secured by Cranmer in November, 1539; and in the patent of that date, which gave to Cromwell control of the printing of the English Bible, the king states that he is granting to the people "the free and liberal use of the Bible in our own maternal English."

This freedom was somewhat abridged in the closing years of Henry's reign, when the tension was tightening between Catholic and Protestant parties within the Church of England. In 1543 an Act for the "advancement of true religion" was passed by Parliament, ordering the destruction of all of Tyndale's translations, forbidding any unauthorized person to read the Bible aloud to others in any public place, and

39

forbidding the private reading of the Bible by all women except noblewomen and gentlewomen, and by all "artificers, apprentices, journeymen, servingmen, yeomen, husbandmen, or laborers."

At Henry's last appearance before Parliament he wept, and moved many in his audience to tears, as he spoke of the failure of his hopes:

Be not judges yourselves of your own fantastical opinions and vain expositions; and although you be permitted to read Holy Scriptures and to have the Word of God in your mother tongue, you must understand it is licensed so to do only to inform your conscience and inform your children and families, not to make Scripture a railing and taunting stock against priests and preachers. I am very sorry to know and hear how irreverently that precious jewel, the Word of God, is disputed, rimed, sung, and jangled in every alehouse and tavern, contrary to the true meaning and doctrine of the same. For of this I am sure, that charity was never so faint among you, and virtuous and godly living was never less used, nor God Himself among Christians never less served. Therefore be in charity one with another, like brother and brother; and love, dread, and serve God, to which I, your Supreme Head and Sovereign Lord, exhort, and require you.

With Henry's death and the accession of Edward the restrictions upon the reading of the English Bible were removed.

3. It was to be expected that English translations of the Bible in the sixteenth century would be heavily loaded with notes and glosses. The Catholic tradition was that Scripture has a fourfold meaning: first, literal or historical; second, allegorical; third, moral; and fourth, anagogical or mystical. To take the most familiar example, "Jerusalem is literally a

city of Palestine, allegorically the Church, morally the believing soul, anagogically the heavenly Jerusalem." John of
Salisbury, English bishop and scholar of the twelfth century,
held that "although the superficial meaning of the letter be
accommodated to a single sense, a multitude of mysteries lie
within; and often allegory edifies faith, and history morals,
and the mystical meaning leads heavenwards in many man-
ners." Because of this principle of the four senses of Scripture, and because of reliance upon the authoritative teaching
of the Church, the glosses and interpretations often seemed
to be more important than the text they undertook to explain. The "bare text" of Scripture was regarded as a dangerous thing, apt to mislead the people. "The letter slayeth,"
a verse from Paul's second epistle to the Corinthians, was
cited in denunciation of those who, like Wycliffe and Tyndale,
insisted that the literal sense of the Scripture is basic.

In 1531 Tyndale declared to Stephen Vaughan, who sought
to induce him to return to England, that he would be satisfied if only a "bare text" might be placed in the hands of
the people. Here are his words, as reported by Vaughan in a
letter to King Henry:

"I assure you," said he, "if it would stand with the king's most
gracious pleasure to grant only a bare text of the scripture to
be put forth among his people, like as is put forth among the subjects of the emperor in these parts, and of other Christian princes,
be it of the translation of what person soever shall please his majesty, I shall immediately make faithful promise never to write
more, nor abide two days in these parts after the same; but immediately to repair into his realm, and there most humbly submit
myself at the feet of his royal majesty, offering my body to suffer
what pain or torture, yea, what death his grace will. so this be ob-

tained. And till that time, I will abide the asperity of all chances, whatsoever shall come, and endure my life in as many pains as it is able to bear and suffer."

Tyndale made no great use of notes. The important thing with him was the text of Scripture itself. "I had perceived by experience," he said, "how that it is impossible to establish the lay people in any truth, except the scripture were plainly laid before their eyes in their mother tongue, that they might see the process, order, and meaning of the text." His marginal notes are brief and comparatively few. The 1526 and 1535 editions of the New Testament have none. It is only the notes on the Old Testament that are sharply critical of his opponents. Those on the New Testament are forthright and clear, but mild in tone. Tyndale could and did use biting language, but this was in his treatises on the current abuses within the Church; except for some of the notes on the Old Testament, he kept sharp comment out of his translation of the Scriptures.

Coverdale had only sixty-six notes for his entire translation—forty-seven in the Old Testament and nineteen in the New—and most of these simply give alternate readings. The notes which he planned for the Great Bible were not published.

Matthew's Bible, the Geneva Bible, and the Bishops' Bible contain more notes than Tyndale. These are of all sorts— textual, expository, doctrinal, and practical. They are anti-papal, not by direct attack, but in the sense that their content is in accord with the principles of the Protestant Reformation. The Rhemish Version has strongly and directly polemical notes, denunciatory of Protestants.

The rules for the making of the King James Version forbade marginal notes, except as these might be required "for the explanation of the Hebrew or Greek words, which cannot without some circumlocution so briefly and fitly be expressed in the text." The spirit of this injunction was 'well observed, yet the marginal notes appended to the King James Version number 6,637 for the Old Testament and 765 for the New Testament. About one third of the notes to the Old Testament and three fourths of the notes to the New Testament give alternative readings; and most of the remainder give a more literal statement of the meaning of one or more of the original words.

4. Shall the English Bible be read, and the English language be used, in the services of the Church? That was a major question, for the language of the Church in the early sixteenth century, as throughout the medieval period, was Latin. Its Bible was the Latin Vulgate; the Mass was said in Latin.

Preaching, of course, was in English; and from the fourteenth century on there was a growing demand for more and better preaching. Lay people were expected to learn the Apostles' Creed, the Ten Commandments, the Pater Noster, and the Ave Maria, and to repeat these in their devotions. Priests were expected, moreover, to explain these to the people in English at least three or four times a year; and a few of the bishops urged that such instruction be given more often, or even on every Lord's Day. Archbishop Thoresby's *Lay Folks' Catechism* (1357) is a manual, in rough English verse, of materials for use in preaching and instruction. John Myrc counselled the priest to inform his flock that

it is much more speedful and meritable to you to say your Pater Noster in English than in such Latin as you do. For when you speak in English, then you know and understand well what you say; and so, by your understanding, you have liking and devotion for to say it.

Necessarily, some English was used in the confessional; and if a person was excommunicated, it was required that the grounds of excommunication should be clearly stated in English, so that the people might understand them. Baptism was valid, even though it be administered by a layman, in case of need, and in English. Bits of English were used in the marriage service.

English materials for instruction in the Christian faith and aids to devotion were contained in the English primers which were in use in the later medieval period. One of these, which belongs to the fourteenth century, is reproduced in G. A. Plimpton's *The Education of Chaucer*. Beginning with the "Christ-cross," it contains the alphabet, the Invocation, the Lord's Prayer, the Ave Maria, the Apostles' Creed, the Ten Commandments, expositions of the seven deadly sins and the seven principal virtues, and translations of 1 Cor. 13, the Beatitudes, and some sayings of Augustine. The *Lay Folks' Mass Book* (about 1300) explains the structure and meaning of the Mass, directs the thoughts of the worshiper, and supplies forms of prayer and devotion. All is cast in rough, jingling English verse, as an aid to the memory; and the reader is advised to "con with-outen boke" so that he may readily use these forms of devotion while the Mass is being said. John Myrc, with respect to the proper use of the Ave Maria, advised:

Teach them to say this in the English tongue, that they may understand what they say. And always, when they come to this word, "God is with thee," that they say it devoutly and with full devotion, not too hastily, to say many Ave's; for it pleaseth our lady more to be greeted devoutly with one Ave, than with many without devotion.

A word of caution is perhaps necessary here. It must not be imagined that the people of England attended Mass in the fourteenth and fifteenth centuries, each with a prayerbook in his hand, in which he could follow the words of the priest. Most people had no books, for they could not afford them before the age of printing. It was only the more wealthy who would possess manuscript translations of the gospels or the psalms or other written aids to devotion. For the people generally Christianity was still an oral religion. They were dependent for their forms of worship upon what they had been taught by word of mouth and could remember. If they could remember nothing else, there was at least the Lord's Prayer.

> If thou can naught read nor say
> Thy pater noster rehearse alway,

says the *Lay Folks' Mass Book*. The same volume urges that if the layman can make no other response in the course of the priest's repetition of the Latin liturgy, he should at least be able to join in the closing petition of the Lord's Prayer:

> but answer at temptacionem
> set libera nos a malo, amen.
> it were no need thee this to ken
> for who con not this are lewed men.

If the worshiper made no other than this one response, and even if he failed to make this, it did not really matter. For the Mass depended in no way upon the participation of the people; they were there to witness it. Even their hearing it was unessential. It was like a stage play which contains a few cues at which the audience is expected to say or do something. The Mass differed from a stage play, however, in that the members of the audience were expected to engage in their own prayers and forms of devotion, while it was being celebrated by the priest and his assistants.

This practice is so far from our present thought of public worship, and the theory underlying it has so important a bearing upon the general problem with which we are dealing, that I quote a more adequate statement from B. L. Manning's compact but thorough study of *The People's Faith in the Time of Wyclif*:

The *Lay Folks' Mass Book* was not a translation of the liturgy. It rested on the theory that the priest and the layman ought to approach God, not by the same, but by different ways. Even their creeds were not identical; the priest used the Nicene formula, the people an English version of the Apostles' Creed. . . . To translate the whole of the liturgy would have been regarded as an act of desecration. Though some of it might be rendered into English with propriety, there was a deep-rooted feeling against any such treatment of the more sacred parts. . . . Alexander VII expressed no new feeling in the Church when, in 1661, he condemned a translation of the whole missal. Only the blasphemous, he thought, could have endeavoured thus "to cast down and trample the majesty of the most sacred rite embodied in the Latin words, and by their rash attempts to expose to the vulgar the dignity of the holy mysteries." The object of the *Lay Folk's Mass Book* was, therefore, not to make the congregation understand what the priest was saying. Two devotions, one lay and one clerical, were to proceed at the same time. According to Lyndwood, who quoted an early fourteenth century writer, the

Canon of the Mass was said in silence *ne impediatur populus orare* [lest the prayers of the people be hindered].[1]

The translation of the Bible into English soon brought about the displacement of Latin as the language of public worship. It led at first to some disorder, for people would take English New Testaments to church and would read from them aloud to their neighbors in the audience while the priest was engaged in the celebration of the Mass; or someone would go to one of the great Bibles chained to its stand by the wall of the church, and read aloud to a growing group, ignoring what the priest was doing. King Henry complained bitterly of such practices, and forbade them in terms such as these:

His Majesty straightly chargeth and commandeth, that no person . . . or persons shall openly read the Bible or the New Testament in the English tongue in any churches or chapels or elsewhere with any loud or high voice, and especially during the time of divine service, or of celebrating and saying of masses; but virtually and devoutly to hear their divine services and masses, and use that time in reading and praying with peace and stillness, as good Christian men used to do.

This disorder was a passing phase, however; quickly, and inevitably, the English Bible began to be read in the proper order of public service in the church, and English became the language of the service itself.

Tyndale showed his regard for the liturgy of the church, and his desire that its Scripture lessons be read in English, by adding to the 1534 and 1535 editions of his New Testament translations of the "epistles" from the Old Testament and Apocrypha that were appointed to be read in the Salisbury

[1] Cambridge Univ. Press. Used by permission of The Macmillan Co.

service book. He translated these directly from the original Hebrew and Greek, and not from the Latin of the missal.

There are records of the use of English in the Mass in the year 1538. In 1543 Convocation ordered

that every Sunday and Holy Day throughout the year the curate of every parish church after the Te Deum and Magnificat should openly read unto the people one chapter of the New Testament in English without exposition, and when the New Testament was finished then to begin the Old.

In 1544 the English Litany was prepared and published, together with an "Exhortation unto Prayer, thought meet by the King's Majesty and his clergy to be read to the people in every church afore Processions." The Exhortation is an excellent little sermon on prayer—why we pray, for what to pray, and how to pray—which goes on to give reasons for the use of the vernacular in prayer:

To the intent, therefore, your hearts and lips may go together in God, that you should use your private prayer in your mother tongue, that you, understanding what you ask of God, may more earnestly and fervently desire the same your hearts and minds agreeing to your mouth and words. . . . Such among the people as have books, and can read, may read them quietly and softly to themself; and in such as cannot read, let them quietly and attentively give audience in time of the said prayers, having their minds erect to Almighty God and devoutly praying in their hearts the same petitions which do enter in at their ears; so that with one sound of the heart and with one accord God may be glorified in his Church.

Here is expressed a theory of public worship far sounder than the medieval theory, and destined to replace it. All of the congregation are to participate, with understanding and with sincerity, in the liturgy of praise and prayer to God. The Litany was reprinted in the King's Primer in 1545.

On Easter Day, April 1, 1548, the Holy Communion was for the first time administered in English; and in May of that year all of the service, including the Mass, was sung in English in St. Paul's, Westminster Abbey, and other London churches. On January 21, 1549, the first *Book of Common Prayer* was adopted; and the issue of the language of public worship was settled. Except for the period under Queen Mary, the Church of England would henceforth use English in its services.

5. The question whether the English Bible should retain the old ecclesiastical words admits of a simple answer in principle: Yes, it should retain all such words as continue to be used in the life of the Church, and can be justified as proper translations of the original Hebrew and Greek. The successive versions of the sixteenth century, leading up to the King James Version, as a matter of fact followed this principle. Stated negatively, ecclesiastical words were not retained which were distinctively Roman, standing for doctrines or practices rejected by the Church of England, or which could not be justified as translations of the original Hebrew or Greek.

For example, Sir Thomas More's accusation that Tyndale was wilfully perverting the Scriptures was based largely upon Tyndale's use of "congregation" instead of "church," "elder" where More wished "priest," "repentance" instead of "penance," and "love" instead of "charity." We shall discuss these terms later; I refer to them now only to illustrate what happened to old ecclesiastical words. Tyndale's suggestion of "congregation" failed, and was replaced by "church" in the Geneva Version and those that followed it. "Elder" was kept because it was a correct translation of the Greek word *presbu-teros,* and "priest" was not. "Repentance" was kept, both as a sound translation of the Greek, and because the Roman Catholic system of penance was rejected. "Love" was kept by all translations up to and including the first edition of the Bishops' Bible. In the second edition of the Bishops' Bible and in the King James Version, it was replaced by "charity" in a bit less than one fourth of the cases of its occurrence. Nineteenth- and twentieth-century revisions have restored "love" in these cases.

6. Tyndale's translation was made directly from the Hebrew and Greek; Coverdale's was based upon the Latin Vulgate. John Rogers, compiling the Bible which was published under his pseudonym of Thomas Matthew, used Tyndale's translations of all books for which these were available, and Coverdale for the remainder, following the principle of using the translations made directly from the original languages as far as he could. The title of the Great Bible, published in 1539, contains the statement "truly translated after the verity of the Hebrew and Greek texts, by the diligent study of divers excellent learned men, expert in the foresaid tongues." Thereafter all authorized versions of the English Bible were based upon the original Hebrew and Greek.

This was not without opposition, however. The Roman Catholics in England, and those of the Church of England who wished to return to the rule of Rome or at least to retain in the Church as much as possible of Roman faith and practice, were insistent upon basing the English version of the Bible, if one had to be made, upon the Latin Vulgate. In the Convocation of 1542 the Great Bible was attacked. When Archbishop Cranmer put the question to the bishops one by one "whether without scandal, error, and manifest offence to Christ's faithful they would vote to retain the Great Bible in the English speech," the majority answered that "the said Bible could not be retained until first duly purged and examined side by side with the [Latin] Bible commonly read in the English Church." It was decided to undertake a revision to bring the Great Bible into accord with the Latin Vulgate, and the various books of the Bible were apportioned for this purpose among the bishops and other clergy who were members of Convocation. Bishop Gardiner presented a list of ninety-nine Latin words and phrases from the Vulgate which, "for the sake of their germane and native meaning and for the majesty of the matter in them contained," should be retained in their Latin form or be rendered into English with the least possible change. The plan came to nothing, for Cranmer consulted the king, who authorized him to announce that it was the royal will and pleasure that the translation be examined by the Universities of Oxford and Cambridge. The bishops protested, but the king's will stood, and the universities let the matter drop.

The Rhemish Version, by Roman Catholic scholars, was based on the Latin. "We translate the old vulgar Latin text," the Preface declares, "not the common Greek text, for these causes . . ."; then follows a detailed list of reasons for so doing. Among them are that the "old vulgar Latin text" is "most ancient"; that it was corrected by Jerome "according to the Greek"; that it "ever since hath been used in the Church's service"; that the Council of Trent had declared it "to be authentical"; that it is the "most grave" and "least partial" of the texts of the holy Scriptures; finally, that "it is not only better than all other Latin translations, but than the Greek text itself, in those places where they disagree," the reason for this being that "most of the ancient heretics were Grecians, and therefore their Scriptures in Greek were more corrupted by them, as the ancient fathers often complain."

7. As was to be expected in view of Tyndale's purpose to make the Scriptures plain in the language of the common people, most of the words that he used were of Anglo-Saxon origin, though he did not hesitate to use terms drawn from French and from Latin. Gardiner's proposal to Latinize the translation was simply one expression of the constant pressure from Catholics, whether Roman or Anglican, to keep as close to the Latin as possible—a pressure that found full expression in the Rhemish Version of 1582, which stayed so close to the Latin as to fail sometimes to be a translation into English. For example, in Eph. 3.6 it reads: "The Gentiles to be co-heirs and concorporate and comparticipant of his promise in Christ Jesus by the Gospel." Sir John Cheke, professor of Greek at Cambridge, went to the other extreme in a translation of Matthew and part of Mark which he made about 1550, excluding all terms derived from the Latin or any other non-English language, and using such renderings as "mooned" for "lunatics," "toller" for "publican," "by-word" for "parable," "crossed" for "crucified," "uprising" for "resurrection," "frosent" for "apostle," and "gainbirth" for "regeneration."

Cheke's work did not influence subsequent versions. On the contrary, both the Bishops' Bible and the King James Version yielded a bit to the pressure of the ecclesiastically sanctioned Latin. The King James Bible owes most to Tyndale, and its next debt is to Geneva; but next to the contribution of Geneva is that of the Rhemish version, from which the King James translators accepted many words and turns of expression that were of Latin origin.

That they should have done this, while in their preface they speak with scorn of the "obscurity" of the "late translation" of "the Papists," is one of the minor ironies of history. The most vigorous defender of the three Protestant versions of the English Bible that were in use in the closing quarter of the sixteenth century—the Great Bible, the Geneva Bible, and the Bishops' Bible—was William Fulke, Master of Pembroke Hall, Cambridge University. His method was eminently fair to his opponents, but singularly devoid of worldly wisdom; for in his major work, entitled *A Defense of the sincere and true Translations of the holie Scriptures into the English tong, against the manifolde cauils, friuolous quarels, and impudent slaunders of Gregorie Martin, one of the readers of Popish diuinitie in the trayterous Seminarie of Rhemes* (1583), he copied, paragraph by paragraph, the book by Martin which he was answering, *A Discoverie of the Manifold Corruptions of the Holy Scriptures by the Heretikes of our daies, specially the English Sectaries, and of their foule dealing herein, by partial & false translations to the aduantage of their heresies, in their English Bibles vsed and authorised since the time of Schisme,* and he thus gave to Martin's work a much larger circulation than it would otherwise have had. As part of the same campaign of defense he published in 1580 a parallel edition of the Rhemish New Testament and the New Testament of the Bishops' Bible, with detailed comments and confutations. This, again, greatly enlarged the circulation of the Rhemish version. Fulkes' parallel edition had so good a sale that it was reprinted in 1589, 1601, 1617, and 1633. Dr. Carleton rightly says that this work "brought under the notice of many an Englishman a version of the Scriptures which otherwise he would not have been likely to concern himself about or even to hear of." But the most ironic touch to the story is that this parallel edition was doubtless used by the King James translators as they undertook the revision of the Bishops' Bible. It was the handiest tool they had; and so Dr. William Fulke, the bitter opponent of the

Rhemish Version, became partly responsible for the influence that it had upon the King James Version.

Yet that influence was not enough to change the predominantly Saxon character of the vocabulary of the King James Version. The often-quoted figures, which I take from Professor Eadie, are that of the words used by Shakespeare about eighty-five per cent are Saxon; by Swift, eight-nine per cent; by Dr. Johnson, almost seventy-five per cent; by Gibbon, about seventy per cent; but that over ninety per cent of the words used in the King James Bible are of Saxon origin.

III

Tyndale and the King James Version

THE English Bible owes more to William Tyndale than
to any other man, not only because he was the first to translate the Bible into English from the original Hebrew and
Greek, but because the basic structure of his translation has
endured through all subsequent changes. "He once for all
determined the style of the English Bible," is the judgment of
Professor J. H. Gardiner at the close of his study of *The Bible
as English Literature.* In the recent volume of essays on *The
Bible in its Ancient and English Versions,* Professor Isaacs of
the University of London says:

> Tyndale's honesty, sincerity, and scrupulous integrity, his
> simple directness, his magical simplicity of phrase, his modest
> music, have given an authority to his wording that has imposed
> itself on all later versions. With all the tinkering to which the New
> Testament has been subject, Tyndale's version is still the basis
> in phrasing, rendering, vocabulary, rhythm, and often in music
> as well. Nine-tenths of the Authorized New Testament is
> still Tyndale, and the best is still his.

The most meticulous study that has yet been made of *The
Literary Lineage of the King James Bible,* by Charles Butterworth, taking account of every minute change in the wording
of forty selections, concludes that "approximately sixty per
cent of the text of the English Bible had reached its final

literary form before the King James Version was produced," and has this to say concerning Tyndale's New Testament:

In it William Tyndale laid an enduring foundation: fully one-third of the New Testament in our Authorized Version is worded just as Tyndale left it; and in the remaining two-thirds, where changes have been made, the sentences follow the general pattern of the underlying structure as Tyndale laid it down.

We shall better understand these statements if we read a few passages from Tyndale's translation. Let us turn first to the familiar passage in John 3.16-21:

For God so loveth the world, that he hath given his only son, that none that believe in him, should perish: but should have everlasting life. For God sent not his son into the world, to condemn the world: but that the world through him, might be saved. He that believeth on him, shall not be condemned. But he that believeth not, is condemned already, because he believeth not in the name of the only son of God.

And this is the condemnation: that light is come into the world, and the men loved darkness more than light, because their deeds were evil. For every man that evil doeth, hateth the light: neither cometh to light, lest his deeds should be reproved. But he that doeth truth, cometh to the light, that his deeds might be known, how they are wrought in God.

There is no need to comment on the changes which the King James Version makes in this passage. They are of minor importance, except perhaps the change from "evil doeth" to "doeth evil"; and not all of them are necessary or better. The outstanding fact is that the translation of these verses is still essentially the work of Tyndale.

Again, let us take a passage from the Sermon on the Mount:

No man can serve two masters. For either he shall hate the one and love the other: or else he shall lean to the one and despise the other: ye cannot serve God and mammon. Therefore, I say unto you, be not careful for your life, what ye shall eat, or what ye shall drink, nor yet for your body, what ye shall put on. Is not the life more worth than meat, and the body more of value than raiment? Behold the fowls of the air: for they sow not, neither reap, nor yet carry into the barns: and yet your heavenly father feedeth them. Are ye not much better than they?

Which of you (though he took thought therefore) could put one cubit unto his stature? And why care ye then for raiment? Consider the lilies of the field, how they grow. They labor not neither spin. And yet for all that I say unto you, that even Solomon in all his royalty was not arrayed like unto one of these. Wherefore if God so clothe the grass, which is to day in the field, and tomorrow shall be cast into the furnace: shall he not much more do the same unto you, o ye of little faith?

Therefore take no thought saying: what shall we eat, or what shall we drink, or wherewith shall we be clothed? After all these things seek the gentiles. For your heavenly father knoweth that ye have need of all these things. But rather seek ye first the kingdom of heaven and the righteousness thereof, and all these things shall be ministered unto you.

This is one of the forty passages which Butterworth has subjected to thorough analysis. It is particularly rich, he shows, in what it has gained through successive revisions, and practically every major version made some contribution to the final result as it appeared in the King James Version.

Yet of the 287 words which the King James rendering contains, 242 are from Tyndale.

Finally, let us turn to Matt. 11.28-30:

Come unto me all ye that labor and are laden, and I will ease you. Take my yoke on you and learn of me, for I am meek and lowly in heart; and ye shall find rest unto your souls. For my yoke is easy, and my burden is light.

In this passage Tyndale supplied the basic translation, and the King James translators improved the rhythm by inserting "heavy" before "laden," substituting "give you rest" for "ease you," and using "upon" for "on."

Butterworth has clearly shown that the language of the King James Verson was not the language of oral speech or of current writing in the period when it was published. And it was not, as is sometimes said, the language of the Elizabethan period. It went back at least seventy-five years, to the time when Tyndale made his translations. It was already, as Butterworth says, "a little old-fashioned by 1611."

We may distinguish, in this respect, between the vocabulary of the King James Version and its style. There is no reason to think that the King James revisers used words in any other meaning than was current in their time; and a comparison with older versions shows that they dropped words that were becoming obsolete. Their vocabulary, on the whole, was used in the sense that this vocabulary had in 1611. But the style of the King James Bible was older. The way in which the words were put together in sentences was not the fashion of their time, but goes back to Tyndale.

And Tyndale's style, in his translation of the New Testament, was more definite and concise than the style current in his day. This is Professor Eadie's opinion, based upon careful study; it is readily confirmed by a comparison of Tyndale's New Testament with the writings and proclamations of King Henry VIII, or with the writings of Sir Thomas More, or even with Tyndale's own writings. The style of the New Testament is more compact and direct; it has shorter sentences; it is not encumbered by the circumlocutions, extended circumstantial clauses, parenthetical observations, and long-winded allusions, which abound in the writing of the time. It is simple, clear, disciplined English prose.

The use of the word "disciplined" to characterize the prose of Tyndale's New Testament may be questioned, I grant. The style is natural and unlabored; it is in some respects even inconsistent and wayward; it is certainly not cribbed by the rules of conscious effort for literary excellence. But it is disciplined by Tyndale's conception of his task, and by his awareness of criticism. This is a translation, not a work of his own, and it must in all respects be true to the original text; it is a translation, moreover, which is from the Greek instead of from the ecclesiastically sanctioned Latin; it is a translation that seeks to put into English the literal, historical meaning of the "bare text," forsaking the accumulated glosses and the tradition of a fourfold sense; it is a translation which must give the truth of the Scriptures, whether or not it is in accord with established doctrines and practices of the Church; it is a translation which is meant for the common people, and must be suited to their understanding; it is a translation, finally, of the Word of God, the gospel which is "the power of God unto salvation to all that believe." Tyndale cannot deal with this as though it were a writing of his own. His style in translating the New Testament is disciplined by the character of the material, by the sincerity of his purpose, and by his awareness that his work will be subject to searching and hostile criticism.

It is idle, therefore, to seek for a period in the development of English literature when the style of the English Bible was generally current among writers. There is no such period. The time of Tyndale comes nearest to it; but the English style of Tyndale's New Testament has a distinct character which is shared by no other book of the time except those which were in some degree dependent upon it.

But we must let Tyndale speak for himself. Here are excerpts from his preface to the 1525 fragment of the New Testament, and from the epistle to the reader appended to the 1526 edition:

I have here translated, brethren and sisters, most dear and tenderly beloved in Christ, the New Testament, for your spiritual edifying, consolation, and solace; exhorting instantly and beseeching those that are better seen in the tongues than I, and that have better gifts of grace to interpret the sense of the Scripture and meaning of the Spirit than I, to consider and ponder my labour, and that with the spirit of meekness; and if they perceive in any places that I have not attained unto the very sense of the tongue, or meaning of the Scripture, or have not given the right English word, that they put to their hands to amend it, remembering that so is their duty to do. For we have not received the gifts of God for ourselves only, or for to hide them; but for to bestow them unto the honouring of God and Christ, and edifying of the congregation, which is the body of Christ.[1]

Them that are learned Christianly I beseech, forasmuch as I am sure, and my conscience beareth me record, that of a pure intent, singly and faithfully, I have interpreted it, as far forth as God gave me the gift of knowledge and understanding, that the

[1] Prologue to the 1525 edition.

rudeness of the work now at the first time offend them not; but that they consider how that I had no man to counterfeit, neither was helped with English of any that had interpreted the same or such like thing in the Scripture beforetime. Moreover, even very necessity, and cumbrance (God is record) above strength, which I will not rehearse, lest we should seem to boast ourselves, caused that many things are lacking which necessarily are required. Count it as a thing not having his full shape, but as it were born before his time, even as a thing begun rather than finished. In time to come (if God have appointed us thereunto) we will give it his full shape, and put out if ought be added superfluously, and add to if ought be overseen through negligence, and will enforce to bring to compendiousness that which is now translated at the length, and to give light where it is required, and to seek in certain places more proper English, and with a table to expound the words which are not commonly used, and show how the Scripture useth many words which are otherwise understood of the common people, and to help with a declaration where one tongue taketh not another; and will endeavour ourselves, as it were, to seethe it better, and to make it more apt for the weak stomachs, desiring them that are learned and able to remember their duty, and to help them thereunto, and to bestow unto the edifying of Christ's body, which is the congregation of them that believe, those gifts which they have received of God for the same purpose.

The grace that cometh of Christ be unto them that love him. Pray for us.[2]

Compendiousness is a word that is not obsolete, yet is little used today. In its place, we speak of conciseness, or terseness, or brevity. Yet more than any of its synonyms, the word compendiousness conveys a sense of the inclusion of large and

[2] Epilogue to the 1526 edition.

weighty matters in a relatively brief summary or statement. It is the word that Tyndale repeatedly uses to express one of his aims. He was conscious of the long-windedness of contemporary speech and writing, and of his own tendency to fall into it when free to let himself go; and he was anxious that the translation of the Scriptures should not suffer from such verbosity. So he kept seeking for more concise renderings; and his final revision of the New Testament shows many places where he has accomplished his purpose "to bring to compendiousness" what he had at first "translated at the length." Examples are: "Blessed are the peace-makers" (Matt. 5.9); the 1526 version had "maintainers of peace." "O ye of little faith" (Matt. 8.26); 1526, "endued with little faith." "In the beginning was the word, and the word was with God, and the word was God" (John 1.1); 1526 has "that word" in all three clauses; and the last clause reads, "God was that word." "Esau, which for one breakfast sold his birthright" (Heb. 12. 16); 1526, "his right that belonged unto him in that he was the eldest brother."

Tyndale never gave up the search for the right word if he had reason to be dissatisfied with the one he had first chosen. For example, in his revision he substitutes "elder" for "seniour" (Acts 14.23); "confessing their sins" for "knowledging their sins" (Matt. 3.6); "salvation" for "health" (Luke 1.77); "convert" for "proselyte" (Acts 2.10); "follow" for "counterfeit" (2 Thess. 3.7); and "chamberlain" for "gelded man" (Acts 8.34).

His changes were not always better; for example, the substitution in Matthew 26.17 of "the first day of sweet bread" for "the first day of unleavened bread."

With all its disciplined restraint the style of Tyndale's New Testament is in one respect a bit wayward. He seems not to care for consistency of rendering; and he varies his translation of some Greek words in a way that sustains the interest of the common reader, but is confusing to a prosaic or pedantic mind. The introductory formula which Luke especially is so fond of using—"and it came to pass"—appears in Tyndale not only in these words, but also as "it happened," "it fortuned," "it chanced," "it followed." The Greek word which is translated "behold" appears also as "lo," "see," "mark," "look," and "take heed." Sometimes Jesus tells a "parable," and sometimes a "similitude," though the Greek word is the same in either case. The scribes and Pharisees who are assailed as "hypocrites" in the twenty-third chapter of Matthew, are twice called "dissemblers" in this same chapter and in translation of the Greek word for "hypocrite." This, however, is an inconsistency which Tyndale corrected in the revised edition, where "hypocrites" is used throughout the chapter and "dissimulation" (verse 28) is changed to "hypocrisy."

In Matt. 24.34-35 Tyndale has: "This generation shall not pass, till all be fulfilled. Heaven and earth shall perish, but my words shall abide." In Mark 13.31-32 and Luke 21.32-33 the same Greek is translated more consistently: "Heaven and earth shall pass, but my words shall not pass."

In Rom. 12.19 and Heb. 10.30, a quotation is made from the Old Testament, the Greek being identical in the two cases. Yet in Romans Tyndale renders it: "Vengeance is mine, and I will reward, saith the Lord"; and in Hebrews he has: "Vengeance belongeth unto me, I will recompense, saith the Lord." That is an inconsistency which was followed by subsequent versions, and still appears in the King James Version. Another inconsistency that still appears in the King James Version is in Matt. 18.33: "Thou shouldest have had compassion on thy fellow, even as I had pity on thee." The words for "compasson" and "pity" are the same in the Greek.

The 1526 edition had Jesus say (John 4.34): "God is a spirit, and they that worship him must honour him in spirit and verity"; the 1534 edition corrected this to read "worship him in spirit and truth." On the other hand Tyndale kept a variation in the translation of the Greek word for "conquer" (Rev. 6.2): "he went forth conquering and for to overcome."

The "field" in which the tares are sown (Matt. 13.24) becomes a "close" when the servants report its condition. The wicked "husbandmen" of Mark 12 are "farmers" in Luke 20, and later appear as "tenants" in both accounts—though the Greek word is the same for all renderings. The fragments that remained after Jesus had fed a multitude are called "gobbets" in Matt. 14 and Mark 6, but in the other accounts in all four Gospels the same Greek word is translated "broken meat." What is called a "pond of fire" in the nineteenth chapter of Revelation becomes a "lake of fire" in the twentieth and twenty-first chapters.

"Did I pill you by any of them which I sent unto you?" asks Paul in 2 Cor. 12.17; and in the next verse he repeats the question with specific reference to Titus: "Did Titus defraud you of anything?" In the Greek the same verb is used in each of the questions. The English verb "pill" is now obsolete, remaining only as the root of the noun "pillage." In 1 Cor. 6.10 Paul includes "pillers" in the list of the unrighteous who shall not inherit the kingdom of God; but just a few verses earlier, in 5.10, the same Greek word is translated "extortioners."

Extreme examples of this disposition of Tyndale to vary his renderings are:

"Give to every man therefore his duty: tribute to whom

tribute belongeth; custom to whom custom is due; fear to whom fear belongeth; honour to whom honour pertaineth." (Rom. 13.7.) In this case no verb except the initial "give" is expressed in the Greek, and he could insert whatever he felt to be appropriate to each clause.

"On the east part three gates, and on the north side three gates, and towards the south three gates, and from the west three gates." (Rev. 21.13.) The reader can hardly know from this that the same form of expression is used in the Greek for each of the four directions.

It is natural to suggest that Tyndale's variations and inconsistencies in the choice of words are due to the hard conditions under which he labored—the "necessity and cumbrance above strength" which "caused that many things are lacking." But there is a deeper and more important reason for these variations. Even if he had been afforded ample time and opportunity for the work, we cannot believe that Tyndale would have translated the New Testament with the mechanical, word-for-word exactness which used to be the ideal of secondary-school teachers.

Tyndale's freedom in the use of words is due rather to the freshness and vitality of his work. His translation is meant for the people. He is determined that they shall have the Word of God in language that they can understand. His mind is set upon the sense of Scripture, and he is bent upon making that plain. He uses the English words, therefore, that come to mind—the natural and appropriate words for the thought or fact which the original language records. If different English words are used in different contexts, or even in the same context, that will but help to convey the meaning. People used the words "field" and "close" in the same sense in common speech—why not in the translation?

The "husbandmen" became "tenants" when they leased the vineyard—why not refer to them as such? Tyndale probably did not even put these questions to himself, or stop to debate whether he could be charged with inconsistency; he just went ahead with his translating, and used the words that he needed to make the meaning clear.

It is easy to make a sort of translation from one language to another by simply writing above each word in the original text an equivalent word in the second language, and then patching these together with whatever minimum of connectives is necessary to make a tolerably intelligible sentence. That is the interlinear, word-for-word method of translation, and it can be employed with full consistency, and consequent impoverishment, by always using the same word for each word in the original. The first Wycliffe version was a translation of this stilted interlinear sort, from the Latin Vulgate; the Rhemish version suffers at many points from its too close adherence to the Latin; the revisers of 1881 and 1901 have given us an excellent translation except that its English style is often hurt by a devotion to "faithfulness," as they called it, which does not throw off the shackles of the interlinear method.

Tyndale was not shackled. He avoided the cramping of interlinear methods on the one hand, and the expansiveness of the traditional glosses and paraphrases on the other. This is not to say that he chose a middle road, looking constantly to the right and left to measure his distance between extremes. No, Tyndale gives the impression, in his translation of the New Testament, of always looking straight ahead. He is concerned with the truth of the Scriptures as set down in the original Greek. He seeks first to determine the literal, historical meaning of the Greek idioms and their use in the sentences; and then he does his best to express that meaning in English idioms and English sentences. Be it granted that he makes some mistakes. That was inevitable. Yet his translation is amazingly sound; it is a natural, free, yet accurate translation by a scholarly and rarely gifted man.

Among Tyndale's mistakes must be listed his use of the names of Christian festivals and holy days for events that took place before these names had acquired that meaning. He even uses these as names for the holy days of the Jews. Thus he says, in John 6.4, that "Easter, a feast of the Jews was nigh"; in Matt. 26.2, "Ye know that after two days shall be Easter, and the son of man shall be delivered up to be crucified"; in Mark 14.16, "The disciples came to the city, and made ready the Easter lamb"; and in Acts 20.6, "we sailed away from Phillippos after the Easter holidays." He not only calls the Jewish Passover Easter but he also calls the day of preparation for the Passover Good Friday, for in Matt. 27.62 we read, "The next day that followeth Good Friday the high priests and Pharisees got themselves to Pilate." In 1 Cor. 16.8 he makes Paul say, "I will tarry at Ephesus until Whitsuntide"; and Rev. 1.10 reads, "I was in the spirit on Sunday." The King James Version eliminated these anachronisms; but through a strange inadvertence it retained one of them. In Acts 12.4 it still says of Herod, who had arrested Peter, that he intended "after Easter to bring him forth to the people." An interesting passage is 1 Corinthians 5.7-8, which reads in Tyndale's version:

Pourge therefore the olde leven, that ye maye be newe dowe, as ye are swete breed. For Christ our esterlambe is offered up for us. Therefore let us keep holy daye, not with olde leven, nether with the leven of maliciousnes and wickednes; but with the swete breed of purenes and truth.

In the King James Version this passage reads:

Purge out therefore the old leaven, that ye may be a new lumpe, as ye are unleavened. For even Christ our Passover is sacrificed for us. Therefore let us keep the Feast, not with old leaven, neither with the leaven of malice and wickedness; but with the unleavened bread of sinceritie and trueth.

In the Rhemish Version this passage is almost unintelligible because of its inclusion of untranslated Latin terms:

Purge the old leaven, that you may be a new paste, as you are azymes. For our Pasche, Christ, is immolated. Therefore let us feast, not in the old leaven, nor in the leaven of malice and wickednes, but in the azymes of sinceritie and veritie.

A peculiar characteristic of Tyndale's style, which has sometimes been attributed to the influence of Luther and German modes of expression, is his fondness for the inverted order of subject and predicate, giving the verb first and following it by the noun which is its subject. In John 9-11, for example, he has such expressions as "brought they," "said some," "that can we not tell," "then rated they him," "went Jesus," "then gathered the high priests." In these three chapters of John, there are twenty-two cases of this inverted order, of which sixteen have been kept in the King James Version. The revisers in 1881 and 1901 kept only five; the Revised Standard Version keeps none. I doubt whether Tyndale would use these inversions if he were writing today. They detract from the simplicity and directness of the translation, add nothing to its dignity, and now avail only to make it appear archaic.

An example of inversion which Tyndale himself corrected in his second edition is Luke 7.18: "And unto John shewed his disciples of all these things." It is typical of much of the careless writing about the English style of the Bible that a recent essayist, quoting this verse as an example of inversion that approaches ambiguity, goes on to say, "This was too much for the Authorized Version." A moment's investigation would have shown him that it was too much for Tyndale, who made the correction in 1534. In subsequent versions the verse read: "And the disciples of John shewed him of all these things." The makers of the King James Version simply accepted what had been the reading for seventy-five years.

Another confusing example of inversion is John 15.19, "therefore hateth you the world." Tyndale did not correct this, and was followed by the Geneva Bible. Coverdale, the Great Bible, and the Bishops' Bible put it in the direct order— "therefore the world hateth you"—and were followed by the King James Version.

Tyndale uses mostly words of Anglo-Saxon strain, but does not hesitate to employ terms of French or Latin origin if these occur to him as a natural expression in English of the thought to be conveyed. In the 1526 edition of the New Testament the plea of the Canaanite woman used a verb derived from the French: "Master, succor me"; but he changed this to "Master, help me" (Matt. 15.25). Familiar as he was with the Latin of the Vulgate and ecclesiastical usage, it was inevitable that he would use words of Latin origin. In contrast with the poor widow, the rich "cast in of their super-fluity" (Mark 12.44); Paul charges the Thessalonians to withdraw "from every brother that walketh inordinately" (2 Thess. 3.6). In the first edition, the men crucified with Jesus are called "malefactors" in Luke 23.39, though they had been described as "evil-doers" in verse 32 of the same chapter; in the second edition "evil-doers" is used in both verses. Those who rely on works of the law are under "malediction" in verse 10 and "the curse" in verse 13 of the third chapter of Galatians, though the Greek word is the same. In Tyndale and all other sixteenth-century versions, John 12.26 reads: "If any man minister unto me, let him follow me, and where I am there shall also my minister be." That sounds a bit strange to us, who have become accustomed to the King James rendering as "serve" and "servant." Yet the fact is that the King James Version translates this Greek verb as "minister" twenty times and as "serve" only nine times.

A letter written by Robert Ridley, chaplain to the Bishop of London, to his friend Henry Gold, chaplain to the Archbishop of Canterbury, dated February 24, almost certainly of the year 1527, condemns the "poisoned and abominable heresies" that he found in Tyndale's New Testament, and goes on to say: "By this translation we shall lose all these Christian words, penance, charity, confession, grace, priest, church, which he alway calleth a congregation. . . . Idolatry calleth he worshipping of images." Thus early began the list of key words which Sir Thomas More accused Tyndale of translating falsely. It would take us too far afield to rehearse the controversy. More's *Dialogue*, Tyndale's *Answer*, and More's *Confutation* are to be found in all university libraries. Fortunately, too, in J. F. Mozley's recent *William Tyndale* we now have for the general reader a competent handling of this, as of other problems with respect to his life and work.

It is enough to say that Tyndale did of set purpose use

other than the established ecclesiastical terms where these were not justified as a translation of the original Greek. More and Tyndale could never find common ground, for More's fixed premise was that the Roman Catholic Church cannot err, whereas Tyndale's conclusion was that it had erred grievously. "Judge, therefore, reader," says Tyndale in his *Answer to Sir Thomas More's Dialogue*, "whether the pope with his be the church; whether their authority be above the scripture; whether all they teach without scripture be equal with the scripture; whether they have erred, and not only whether they can." In the end Tyndale's word "elder" was kept as the translation of *presbuteros,* and the word "priest" was limited to the translation of *hiereus,* because that is the correct meaning of these Greek terms. For the same reason "penance" was displaced by "repentance" and "do penance" by "repent." With respect to "confession" and "grace" Tyndale was misrepresented by More. Tyndale retains "confess" in fifteen out of twenty-four passages, and "grace" in more than a hundred. He used "favour" instead of "grace" in twenty passages in his first edition, and reduced these to five in the second edition. "Sacrament" is a word that he did not use, but no other English version made by translation from the original Greek uses this word. The Greek term is *mysterion,* which the Latin Vulgate translated by *mysterium* in nineteen cases and by *sacramentum* in eight. Modern translations from the Vulgate by Ronald Knox and by the scholars working under the Confraternity of Christian Doctrine do not use the word "sacrament" in these passages. Tyndale uses "idolatry" or "idolaters" six times, and "worshipping of images" or "worshipper of images" six times; this seems to be simply one of his characteristic variations of rendering.

Tyndale translated the Greek word *ecclesia,* as applied to

those who are called to follow Christ, by the English word "congregation" rather than by "church." He did this, he tells us, because the word "church" had been so misused that in the minds of the people generally it stood for the ecclesiastical hierarchy rather than for the whole body of Christian believers.

Inasmuch as the clergy . . . had appropriate unto themselves the term that of right is common unto all the whole congregation of them that believe in Christ, . . . making them understand by this word *church* nothing but the shaven flock of them that shore the whole world, therefore in the translation of the New Testament, when I found this word *ecclesia,* I interpreted it by this word *congregation.*

He was followed in this by Coverdale and Cranmer. The Geneva Bible used both "church" and "congregation," with about equal frequency. The Bishops' Bible used "church" throughout, except in two passages. One is Heb. 12.23, referring to "the congregation of the first-born, which are written in heaven." The other, of notable significance, is the Lord's word to Peter in Matt. 16.18: "I say also unto thee that thou art Peter; and upon this rock I will build my congregation." The use made of this text by the Roman Catholic Church may explain Archbishop Parker's leaving it as it had appeared in Tyndale, Coverdale, the Great Bible, and the Geneva Bible. The King James Version uses the word "congregation" only once, and then of the assembly in a Jewish synagogue (Acts 13.43). The march of events in sixteenth-century England made it seem better to redeem the old word "church" than to forsake it for the word "congregation."

The basic principle and ultimate motive of both the Christian gospel and the Christian ethic is love. "God is love," we are taught in the New Testament. "God so loved the world that he gave his only Son, that whoever believes in him should not perish but have eternal life." God shows his love for us in that "while we were yet sinners Christ died for us." "If God so loved us, we also ought to love one another." "He who abides in love abides in God, and God abides in him." When asked which is the great commandment, Jesus answered: "Thou shalt love the Lord thy God with all thy heart, and with all thy soul, and with all thy mind. This is the first and great commandment, and the second is like it: Thou shalt love thy neighbor as thyself." These are familar texts. I have quoted them because we need to keep in mind as we go on to discuss the translation of the Greek word for love— *agape*—that we are dealing here not with a mere exhortation to feeling and action, or even with a statement of human duty, but with the ultimate grounding of human duty and destiny in the very nature and eternal purpose of God. Whatever would tend to separate human love from divine love, or to weaken the essential connection between the Christian ethic and the Christian gospel, is wrong.

There are three Greek words for love, two of which need not concern us here. *Eros* and its verb *erao*, which refer primarily to sexual love, do not appear in the New Testament. *Philia* and its verb *phileo*, which refer primarily to personal friendship, occur only twenty-six times; and the noun *philos*, which means friend, occurs twenty-nine times. But the noun *agape* is used 114 times, the verb *agapao* 136 times, and the adjective *agapetos* 62 times—a total of 312 occurrences. In the King James Version the verb is translated "love" in 130 cases, and its participle "beloved" in six cases. The adjective is translated "beloved" 59 times and "dear" three times. But a strange thing has happened to the noun. Excluding two cases where its plural is used in the sense of love feasts, there remain 112 occurrences. Of these 85 are translated "love," but in 26 the rendering is "charity," and in one case a prepositional phrase is rendered by the adverb "charitably."

Except in the one case when he too uses the adverb "charitably" Tyndale always translated *agape* by the word "love." When rebuked by More, who wished to retain the Latin-derived, ecclesiastically sanctioned word "charity," Tyndale answered that "charity is not known English, in that sense which *agape* requireth," and that in common use it means either almsgiving or patience and mercifulness in the judgment of others. He called attention, finally, to the fact that "charity" is a noun that has no correlative verb or adjective, as *agape* has. "I say not, charity God, or charity your neighbor; but, love God, and love your neighbor."

In his translation of *agape* by "love," Tyndale was followed by all sixteenth-century versions up to 1568—Coverdale, Matthew, Taverner, the Great Bible, and the Geneva Bible. He was followed by the Bishops' Bible also, except for one verse, Rom. 13.10, where the word "charity" was introduced. The result was a bit absurd, for the preceding verse ends with the second great commandment, and the change causes the passage to close with a startling shift of language. Rom. 13.8-10 reads as follows in the Bishops' Bible:

Owe nothing to no man, but to love one another: For he that loveth another hath fulfilled the law. For this: Thou shalt not commit adultery, thou shalt not kill, thou shalt not steal, thou shalt not bear false witness, thou shalt not lust and if there be any other commandment it is comprehended in this saying: namely, thou shalt love thy neighbor as thyself. Charity worketh no ill to his neighbor, Therefore the fulfilling of the law is charity.

In 1572 there came a real break. The advocates of Catholic Latinity had in some way gathered strength, for in the second edition of the Bishops' Bible, published in that year, the word "charity" is substituted for "love" in thirty-two cases. The word "love" remained in the other cases, and of course in the translation of the verb *agapao*.

When the committee appointed by King James revised the Bishops' Bible to make the Authorized Version of 1611, they restored the word "love" in six out of the thirty-two cases. But they kept the word "charity" in twenty-six cases. Just why they did that, we can only conjecture. Certainly there is no clear reason, no principle of literature or logic or ethics or theology, to explain why the word *agape* should be rendered as "charity" in these twenty-six instances, while it is translated "love" in eighty-five other instances of generally similar context.

Even an attempt to attribute the twenty-six divergent cases to differences in the Latin Vulgate, fails to explain them. There are three Latin words for "love"—*amor, dilectio,* and *caritas*. The first of these is never used to represent *agape* in the Latin New Testament; *dilectio* is used in about one fifth of the cases of its occurrence, and *caritas* is used in the rest. The Rhemish Version, which was made by translation from the Latin, reproduces this divergence. It always uses the English word "love" for *dilectio,* and "charity" for *caritas.* The distinction was not justified by anything in the original Greek; but the procedure of the Rhemish translators was at least consistent. It resulted in such translations as these: "My dearest, let us love one another, because charity is of God. . . . He that loveth not, knoweth not God; because God is charity." (1 John 4.7-8.)

But in this matter the King James translators are no more

consistent with the Latin than with the Greek. Of the 26 cases where they use "charity" three have *dilectio* in the Latin and 23 *caritas*. Of the 85 cases where they use "love" 20 have *dilectio* and 65 *caritas*.

The truth is that it is futile to look for a distinction here, for no valid distinction can be found. If Jerome had any distinction in his mind when he used the Latin word *dilectio* to represent *agape* in a few cases and *caritas* in the rest, it was a distinction that he did not get from the Greek. There is evidence, moreover, that no such distinction was maintained in the usage of the English Church in the 1570's. The *Catechism* by Alexander Nowell, Dean of St. Paul's, sanctioned by the Convocation of Canterbury, written in Latin and then translated into English by Thomas Norton, was published in both languages in 1570. It shows that in Latin *caritas, dilectio,* and even *amor* were used interchangeably, and so were "charity" and "love" in English. Take, for example, this clause from the answer to the question regarding our duty toward Christ: "That we with all our affection, love, esteem, and embrace Christ our Savior, which showed us such dear love while we were yet his enemies, as his most entire love toward us could not possibly be increased." In the Latin of this passage the verb for love was *amo,* and the verb for esteem *diligo;* while the first noun for love was *caritas,* and the second *amor.*

The distribution of the 26 cases in which the King James Version kept the word "charity" which had been introduced by an unknown reviser of the Bishops' Bible, is peculiar. There are no such cases before 1 Cor. 8.1. Eleven of the 26 cases are in 1 Corinthians, six in the Pastoral epistles, and four in the epistles of Peter; the other five are one each in Colossians, 1 Thessalonians, 2 Thessalonians, 3 John, and Revelation.

Eight of them are in one chapter, 1 Cor. 13. None of them are in 1 John, the epistle of love.

These cases represent a compromise between the clear-cut position of the earlier translators, from Tyndale to the Geneva Bible, and the pressure of the Catholic party for the term derived from the Latin and established in ecclesiastical usage. Such a compromise would not be uncongenial to Archbishop Parker, who had to make many compromises and who accomplished a great work because he could do it without obvious loss of principle. No records have come down to us, and we can only conjecture, as I have said. The one change to the word "charity" which was made in the first edition of the Bishops' Bible (Rom. 13.10) looks now like a sort of trial balloon, to test how the wind was blowing. The test seems to have been satisfactory enough that the second edition of the Bishops' Bible made the change in thirty other places.

As to why these particular places should have been chosen for the change to "charity," and why the King James revisers should have kept twenty-six of them, we can only guess. Two guesses may be not wholly wrong. 1 Cor.13 was one of the most familiar parts of the New Testament; English versions of it had appeared in primers and aids to devotion; many people doubtless had committed it to memory, both in Latin and in English. Here the word "charity" was established in the public mind. And it was perhaps natural, too, to retain the Latin-derived word in the Pastoral epistles, as an echo of the language of the confessional.

The Revised Versions of 1881 and 1901 restored the word "love" in the passages where it had been displaced by "charity," and the translation of *agape* is now consistent throughout the New Testament. Even the recent Catholic translations from the Vulgate by Father Knox and the Confraternity of Christian

Doctrine break away from the supposed distinction between *dilectio* and *caritas;* and they use "love" as the translation for *caritas* in the crucial passages contained in the epistles of John.

A recent writer on Tyndale's use of English says: "Whether or no 'love' is the better translation, it is an abrupt little word, and undoubtedly 'charity' reads better in the context. But this was a matter of principle, not of taste."[3] The argument that we should use "charity" because it is more rhythmic is trivial compared to the principle that requires the use of the word "love."

It chances that concerning this principle we have a statement by Bishop Westcott himself; and we may well conclude by quoting it:

Many feel still a natural regret that the word "charity" has no place in the Revised Version. . . . Charity is indeed a word of most touching sweetness. It can never lose its position in the vocabulary of Christian graces. But to retain it in the New Testament is to hide the source of its strength and glory. No one, as far as I am aware, ever proposed to adopt into our English Version the Latin rendering, *Deus est caritas,* "God is charity," which stands in the Rhemish translation; and yet no loss to Christian morality could be greater than the separation of the grace from its Divine archetype. The strength of the Christian character lies in the truth that he who has love shares according to his measure in the Divine nature. Thus by using in English different words to express the relation of God to man and of man to men, calling the one "love" and the other "charity," where the original Scriptures use one word only to describe in this aspect the relations of God to man, and of man to God, and of man to man, we weaken the bond which unites the human and Divine,

[3] G. D. Bone, in S. L. Greenslade, *The Work of William Tyndale,* p. 59.

we remove the revelation of that harmony which exists, according to the idea of creation, between man made in the image of God and God Himself. . . . When we say "God is love" (I John 4.16), and "charity never faileth" (I Corinthians 13.8), we have lost the connection between the two thoughts; we have lost, that is, a link which unites by an essential bond the teaching of St. John and St. Paul.

Am I not then right in believing that when once the facts are seen in their fulness, the English reader will recognize his gain in having the greatest of human graces indissolubly connected with the very being of God, and seen to be eternal because He is eternal.

IV

The King James Version in Three Centuries

THE King James Version of the Bible, published in 1611, gradually displaced the Geneva Bible in popular use, and from the middle of the seventeenth century until the close of the nineteenth its position was undisputed as *The* English Bible. This was due not merely to the fact that it was the only Authorized Version of that period but to its merit as a translation and as English literature. It is "a miracle and a landmark," says the essay dealing with it in the recent volume edited by Principal Robinson. Professor Eadie, one of its most discerning critics, said:

While it has the fulness of the Bishops' [Bible] without its frequent literalisms or its repeated supplements, it has the graceful vigor of the Genevan, the quiet grandeur of the Great Bible, the clearness of Tyndale, the harmonies of Coverdale, and the stately theological vocabulary of the Rheims.

The revisers of the 1870's in the preface to their edition of 1881 record their admiration for the excellence of the King James Version—for "its simplicity, its dignity, its power, its happy turns of expression, its general accuracy, . . . the music of its cadences, and the felicities of its rhythm." To this may be added the recent verdict of Sir Frederic Kenyon:

It is the simple truth that, as literature, the English Authorized Version is superior to the original Greek. It was the good fortune of the English nation that its Bible was produced at a time when the genius of the language for noble prose was at its height, and when a natural sense of style was not infected by self-conscious scholarship. The beauty of the language commended the teaching of the sacred books and made them dear to the heart of the people, while it made an indelible and enduring impression alike on literature and on popular speech.[1]

If it is asked to what human factors the excellence of the King James Version is to be attributed, the answer is, first, that it was a revision rather than a wholly new translation, and that it stood at the close of eighty-five years of repeated revision of the English Bible. It owes much to this prior work. The translators kept felicitous turns of phrase and apt expressions, from whatever source, which had stood the test of public usage. This was the first version, moreover, to be produced by the full and well-ordered use of the method of scholarly conference. Each of the versions prior to 1560 had been the work of one man; the Geneva Bible and the Rhemish New Testament were produced by small groups of scholars; for the Bishops' Bible Archbishop Parker enlisted the services of sixteen men, but there was no face-to-face discussion of the problems encountered in the work of translation, and their individual contributions were not properly edited. The King James translators, for the first time, used the method of conference between a number of scholars, with provision for individual work, group discussion, correspondence between groups, and final integration by a representative and respon-

[1] *The Story of the Bible* (E. P. Dutton & Co.). Copyright 1937 by Sir Frederic Kenyon.

sible editorial committee. Again, in spite of the king's impatient urging they did not hurry the work but took sufficient time to do it well. They were appointed and organized in 1604, and the book was published in 1611; they spent at least three years in the actual labor, according to Dr. Myles Smith's statement in the preface.

More important than any of these matters of method was the character of the men themselves. They were competent scholars, chosen from the best that the Church of England had in their day. They were men of devout religious faith, evangelical and catholic in the true sense of these terms. And they learned to work together. There were Puritans among them but no nonconformists. One Hebrew scholar of great repute was not invited to serve because of his notorious self-will and inability to work with others. He retaliated, when the work was published, by sending word to the king that he "had rather be rent in pieces with wild horses" than consent that so "ill-done" a version of the Bible be urged upon the churches.

It is most unfortunate that the publishers of the King James Bible have ceased to publish the preface entitled "The Translators to the Reader," and have continued to publish the adulatory dedication to King James. The dedication is worse than useless; it conveys to the modern reader an impression of fawning. It was meant for the king, and might well have been buried with him. But the preface was meant for the readers of the Bible, and it is still important. If it were published in every edition of the King James Bible, as the translators meant that it should be, the character of their work would be better understood, and the King James Bible would be protected from some of the misconceptions that cluster about it.

The preface is long, and most of it is devoted to a statement of the reasons which justify the translation of the Scriptures into the language of the people. The Bible itself and the early fathers of the Church are quoted in opposition to the attitude toward vernacular translations into which the Church of Rome had fallen. There is no need for us here to review this clearly reasoned and well sustained argument. It is a proper conclusion to the sixteenth-century battle for the vernacular which has already been described.

Let us review briefly, however, what the translators say about the motives, purpose, and method of their work. It is best to let them speak for themselves. The following is an abstract of passages from the beginning and toward the end of the preface:

Zeal to promote the common good, whether it be by devising anything ourselves, or revising that which hath been laboured by others, deserveth certainly much respect and esteem, but yet findeth but cold entertainment in the world. It is welcomed with suspicion instead of love, and with emulation instead of thanks: and if there be any hole left for cavil to enter, (and cavil, if it do not find a hole, will make one) it is sure to be misconstrued, and in danger to be condemned. . . . Was there ever anything projected, that savoured any way of newness or renewing, but the same endured many a storm of gainsaying, or opposition? . . .

We are so far off from condemning any of their labours that travailed before us in this kind, either in this land or beyond sea, either in King Henry's time . . . or Queen Elizabeth's of ever renowned memory, that we acknowledge them to have been raised up of God, for the building and furnishing of his Church, and that they deserve to be had of us and of posterity in everlasting remembrance. . . . Blessed be they, and most honoured be their name, that break the ice, and giveth onset upon that which helpeth forward to the saving of souls. Now what can be more available thereto, than to deliver God's book unto God's people in a tongue which they understand? . . . Yet for all that, as nothing is begun and perfected at the same time, and the later thoughts are thought to be the wiser: so, if we building upon their foundation that went before us, and being holpen by their labours, do endeavor to make that better which they left so good; no man, we are sure, hath cause to mislike us; they, we persuade ourselves, if they were alive, would thank us. . . .

Truly (good Christian Reader) we never thought from the beginning, that we should need to make a new Translation, nor yet to make of a bad one a good one, . . . but to make a good one better, or out of many good ones, one principal good one, not justly to be excepted against; that hath been our endeavor, that our mark. To that purpose there were many chosen, that were greater in other men's eyes than in their own, and that sought the truth rather than their own praise. . . . If you ask what they had before them, truly it was the Hebrew text of the Old Testament, the Greek of the New. . . . These tongues therefore, the Scriptures we say in those tongues, we set before us to translate, being the tongues wherein God was pleased to speak to his Church by his Prophets and Apostles. Neither did we run over the work with that posting haste that the Septuagint did, if that be true which is reported of them, that they finished it in 72 days; neither were we barred or hindered from going over it again, . . . neither . . . were we the first that fell in hand with translating the Scripture into English, and consequently destitute of former helps. . . . None of these things: the work hath not been huddled up in 72 days, but hath cost the workmen, as light as it seemeth, the pains of twice seven times seventy two days and more. . . .

Neither did we think much to consult the Translators or Commentators, Chaldee, Hebrew, Syrian, Greek, or Latin, no nor the Spanish, French, Italian, or Dutch; neither did we disdain to revise that which we had done, and to bring back to the anvil that which we had hammered: but having and using as great helps as were needful, and fearing no reproach for slowness, nor coveting praise for expedition, we have at the length, through the good hand of the Lord upon us, brought the work to that pass that you see. . . .

The King James Version as printed today differs in many respects from the original as published in 1611. Almost from the first, changes in spelling, punctuation, and the use of italics began to be made as successive editions appeared. The most thorough reshaping of the printed text along these lines, together with a recasting of marginal references, notes, and page headings, was made by Dr. Benjamin Blayney, of Oxford University, in 1769. One peculiar defect which has never been remedied is that the King James Version contains no paragraph marks beyond the twentieth chapter of Acts. The division of the text into paragraphs abruptly ceases at just the point where it begins to be most needed, with the epistles of Paul. No reason can be given for this; it simply looks as if the printing had been hurried toward the end. Probably it makes little difference, for the printing of each verse as a distinct paragraph in the King James Version has so obscured the division into paragraphs according to the sense that most people are not aware that the Version has paragraph marks up to the end of Acts 20.

The King James Version was severely criticized by various scholars in the 1650's, and in 1653 a bill was brought before the Long Parliament expressing the fear that revisions and new translations might be made and published by individuals, "which if it should be done on their own heads, without due care for the supervising thereof by learned persons sound in the fundamentals of the Christian religion, might be a precedent of dangerous consequence, emboldening other to do the like." A committee of scholars was appointed to examine any proposed revision, without whose authority it could not appear. In 1657 a committee was appointed to undertake revision of the King James Version if it should be deemed necessary, but the dissolution of Parliament put an end to this proposal.

For two centuries there were no more official attempts to revise the King James Version. Not until 1856 was the matter seriously discussed in Convocation or in Parliament.

There were, of course, various individual efforts to revise the King James Version or to produce a new translation. Some of these were in the interest of Unitarianism or Universalism; a larger number may be grouped as "immersionist" versions, because of their attempt to displace the word "baptize" by the word "immerse" or "dip." Others were frank attempts to bring the New Testament up to date, and make it speak the language of the day. The latter are worth examining, not because of their importance, but precisely because they failed to be of any importance whatever.

In 1729 William Mace, a Presbyterian minister, published *The New Testament in Greek and English . . . corrected from the Authority of the most Authentic Manuscripts.* His corrections of the Greek text were in the direction of sound scholarship; but his English version was too obvious an attempt to copy "the humour of the age"—the pert, colloquial style which was then fashionable. Here are some examples:

"When ye fast, don't put on a dismal air as the Hypocrites do" (Matt. 6.16); "'tis the overflowing of the heart that the mouth dischargeth" (Matt. 12.34); "the people reprimanded them to make them hold their tongue, but they bawl'd out the more, Have mercy on us" (Matt. 20.31); "and the domestics slapt him on the cheeks" (Mark 14.65); "eating and drinking, marriages and matches, was the business" (Luke 17.27); "If any man thinks it would be a reflection upon his manhood to be a stale bachelor" (1 Cor. 7.1); "Social affection is patient, is kind" (1 Cor. 13.4); and "if you should respectfully say to the suit of fine cloths, sit you there, that's for quality" (Jas. 2.3).

Fashions change, in literature as in amusements and in dress. The easy familiarity which Mace tried to practice was displaced by the dignified style of the age of Dr. Samuel Johnson. In 1768 Dr. Edward Harwood published *A Liberal Translation of the New Testament; Being an Attempt to translate the Sacred Writings with the same Freedom, Spirit, and Elegance, with which other English Translations from the Greek Classics have lately been executed.* In the preface Dr. Harwood asks the reader to bear in mind that "this is not a verbal translation, but a *liberal* and *diffusive* version of the sacred classics, and is calculated to answer the purpose of an explanatory paraphrase as well as a free and elegant translation."

He states his belief that *"such* a Translation of the New Testament might induce persons of a liberal education and polite state to peruse the sacred volume, and that such a version might prove of signal service to the cause of truth, liberty, and Christianity, if men of cultivated and improved minds, especially YOUTH, could be allured by the innocent stratagem of a *modern style,* to read a book, which is now, alas! too generally neglected and disregarded by the young and gay, as a volume containing little to amuse and delight."

Dr. Harwood's translation is what one would expect from the expansive, condescending dignity of the preface. The following passage is typical (Matt. 20.20-28):

Then the wife of Zebedee, imagining that after his resurrection the grand temporal kingdom of the Messiah would be erected, approached him, conducting her two sons—and discovered, by her ceremonious address, that she was desirous to solicit a favour from him. Jesus said to her—What kindness is it you appear so desirous to obtain?—She replied—These my two sons have been your faithful and inseparable companions—I entreat you that you would advance them, in the kingdom you are going to establish, to two of the most elevated and illustrious stations. Jesus said—You discover great ignorance of the true nature of my kingdom by such a request—Are you able to endure the trials, in which I am going to be involved?—are you able to sustain that dreadful shock of sufferings, which I must soon support?— Our fortitude is equal to it—they replied. He continued—The same human miseries, indeed, that will soon seize me, will also invade you! and the same sufferings and persecutions that will befall me, will also assail you—but it is not in my power to dispose of the highest dignities in my future kingdom—that power is solely vested in the supreme father of all, who will confer them on persons of superior virtue and the sublimest attainments. The other ten disciples, who had heard this conversation, conceived the most violent resentment against the two brothers for this ambitious attempt to supplant them. Jesus, conscious of the aspiring views by which they were actuated, collected them into a body, and thus addressed them—Potent monarchs among the Heathens, you know, rule their subjects with an absolute and despotic tyranny—and the princes and governours of the several states and communities among them usurp and exercise a sovereign and uncontrolable authority in their dominions. But such a lust of domination and fondness of power shall never possess your bosoms —For among you he that is the humblest shall be the greatest: And he who is desirous to fill the most elevated and illustrious station among you, let him practice the most kind submission, and the most humane condescention, in humble imitation of the son of man, who came not into this world to make mankind his vassals, and to enjoy the magnificence and homage of a court—but to do the kindest and most condescending offices, and to surrender up his life, that he might rescue men from vice and destruction.

An American production of no less pretension was *A New and Corrected Version of the New Testament,* by Rodolphus Dickinson, published at Boston in 1833. The preface to this volume is an astonishing exhibition of conceit. The author condemns the "quaint monotony and affected solemnity" of the King James Version, with its "frequently rude and occasionally barbarous attire"; and he declares his purpose to adorn the Scriptures with "a splendid and sweetly flowing diction" suited to the use of "accomplished and refined persons." He asks:

Why should the inestimable gift of God to man, be proffered in a mode that is unnecessarily repulsive? Why should the received translation be permitted to perpetuate, to legalize, and almost to sanctify, many and unquestionable defects? . . . Why should the Christian scriptures be divested even of decent ornament? Why should not an edition of the heavenly institutes be furnished for the reading-room, saloon, and toilet, as well as for the church, school, and nursery? for the literary and accomplished gentleman, as well as for the plain and unlettered citizen? . . . Why should the Bible be stationary, amid the progress of refinement and letters? Why, in antique fashion, should it remain solitary, in the enchanting and illimitable field of modern improvements?

The text of Mr. Dickinson's translation is not as bad as the preface leads us to expect and is much closer to the original than Harwood's paraphrase; but it is erratic, to say the least. Here are some of its renderings: "And it happened, that when Elizabeth heard the salutation of Mary, the embryo was joyfully agitated." (Luke 1.41.) "Seek first the empire of God, and the integrity he requires, and all these things shall be superadded to you." (Matt. 6.33.) "Be not therefore inquisitive, what you shall eat, or what you shall drink; nor be in unquiet suspense." (Luke 12.29.) "And his master said to him, Well-done, good and provident servant! you was faithful in a limited sphere. I will give you a more extensive superintendence; participate in the happiness of your master." (Matt. 25.21.) "Festus declared with a loud voice, Paul, you are insane! Multiplied research drives you to distraction." (Acts 26.24.)

He came to Jesus by night, and said to him, Teacher, we know what thou art an instructor emanated from God; for no one can achieve these miracles which thou performest, unless God be with him. Jesus answered and said to him, Indeed, I assure you, that except a man be reproduced, he cannot realize the reign of God. Nicodemus says to him, How can a man be produced when he is mature? Can he again pass into a state of embryo, and be produced? Jesus replied, I most assuredly declare to you, that unless a man be produced of water and of the Spirit, he cannot enter the kingdom of God. (John 3.2-5.)

The translations by Mace, Harwood, and Dickinson deserve the fate which they have met—to be forgotten save as someone disinters them "to point a moral or adorn a tale." The moral is that we should learn from them the folly of what Archbishop Trench called "the worship of the fleeting present, of the transient fashions of the hour in language, with contempt of that stable past which in all likelihood will be the enduring future, long after these fashions have passed away and are forgotten."

A sounder method was followed by Noah Webster, author of the famous *American Dictionary of the English Language,* which still lives and is authoritative, having been repeatedly revised and expanded, first as *Webster's Unabridged,* then as *Webster's International,* and finally as the bulky volume which is now in general use, the Second Edition of *Webster's New International Dictionary.* Webster devoted a long life to the study of the English language. His *Speller,* published in 1783, was used as a schoolbook for more than a century, and attained a sale of more than 60,000,000 copies. His first dictionary was published in 1806, and the larger American dictionary in 1828. Webster then devoted himself to what he called "the most important undertaking" of his career, the attempt "to render the English version of the Bible more useful, by correcting a few obvious errors and removing some obscurities." His revised version of the Bible, entitled *The Holy Bible, containing the Old and New Testaments, in the Common Version, with Amendments of the language* was published in 1833.

Unlike Dickinson, whose work was published in the same year, Webster had high regard for the King James Version. Its language, he said, "is in general correct and perspicuous; the genuine popular English of Saxon origin; peculiarly adapted to the subjects, and in many passages, uniting sublimity with beautiful simplicity." But he called attention to the fact that

in the lapse of two or three centuries changes have taken place, which, in particular passages, impair the beauty, in others, obscure the sense, of the original languages. Some words have fallen into disuse; and the signification of others, in current popular use, is not the same now as it was when they were introduced into the version. . . . Whenever words are understood in a sense different from that which they had when introduced, and different from that of the original languages, they do not present to the reader the *Word of God*. . . . A version of the scriptures for popular use should consist of words expressing the sense which is most common in popular usage, so that the first ideas suggested to the reader should be the true meaning of such words according to the original languages. . . . That many words in the present version fail to do this, is certain. My principal aim is to remedy this evil.

As was to be expected of a dictionary maker Webster began with an Introduction in which he carefully listed and explained the alterations he had made in the English text of the King James Version. There were some one hundred and fifty words and phrases which he found to be erroneous or misleading, and which he corrected in the various passages where they appeared. Practically all of these have been changed by later revisers also, who found his judgment sound as to the need of change, and in most cases accepted the corrections he proposed. He substituted "who" for "which," when it refers to persons; and "its" for "his," when it refers to things. He used "Be not anxious" for "Take no thought"; "food" for "meat"; "ask" for "demand"; "hinder" for the obsolete sense of "let"; and various words appropriate to the context for "prevent" in its obsolete sense of "go before." He used the term "Holy Spirit" instead of "Holy Ghost." He corrected the grammatical error in the King James rendering of Jesus' question at Caesarea Philippi (Matt. 16.13), "Whom do men say that I the Son of man am?" making it read "Who do men say that I the Son of man am?" Where Paul wrote "would that," the King James Version makes him say "would to God," and in fourteen cases where he wrote "be it not so" the King James Version reads "God forbid"; Webster removed the insertion of the name of God from both of these expressions. By a printer's error the original edition of the King James Version (Matt. 23.24) had "strain at a gnat" instead of "strain out a gnat"; and by some odd perversity of human nature this misprint has never been corrected in any subsequent edition of the King James Version, and some men are to be found who will even argue that "strain at" is a correct translation. Webster knew better, and has an interesting note upon the point. His biographer is mistaken, however, when he claims that by substituting "strain out" for "strain at" Webster "for the first time in an English Bible rendered Jesus' saying as he said it, and corrected the figure of speech." The fact is that all of the earlier English versions, from Tyndale to the Bishops' Bible, used the expression "strain out a gnat." The King James Version stands alone in this error.

As far as it went, Noah Webster's revision of the English Bible was sound. It pointed the way that revision should take in matters of English usage. For a time it was used in many Congregational churches; a second edition was published in 1841, and three editions of his revision of the New Testament were printed in 1839, 1840, and 1841. But then it faded from public view, and now it is almost forgotten. It made too few amendments to challenge attention; it was not adopted for general use in the public worship of the churches; and it did not go far enough, in that it was based almost wholly upon English usage, and did not push back of this to the problems with respect to the Greek text of the New Testament that were emerging in the 1830's and 1840's. Perhaps Webster's biographer is justified, however, in his conjecture that President Woolsey, President Dwight, and Professor Day, the Yale members of the American Bible Revision Committee in the 1870's and 1880's "may well have derived their insistence on Webster-like emendations from their use of Webster's edition."

The basic factor in any translation of the New Testament is, of course, the Greek text; and a compelling reason for revision appears where it is shown to have been in error. By the middle of the nineteenth century the study of the Greek manuscripts of the New Testament had shown beyond question that the King James Version was based upon a Greek text that contained the accumulated errors of fifteen centuries of manuscript copying. It was essentially the Greek text as edited by Beza, who closely followed the text issued by Erasmus, which had been based upon a mere handful of late medieval manuscripts. The earliest and best of the eight manuscripts which Erasmus consulted was from the tenth century, and he made the least use of it because it differed most from the commonly received text; Beza had access to two manuscripts of great value, dating from the fifth and sixth centuries, but he made very little use of them because they differed from the text published by Erasmus.

In 1627, only sixteen years after the publication of the King James Version, a beautiful manuscript of the Bible, the

Codex Alexandrinus, written in the first half of the fifth century, came to England, a gift to the King from the Patriarch of Constantinople. This greatly stimulated interest in the search for other ancient manuscripts of the Bible, and in the collation of their various readings. I shall not undertake to sketch the history of the movement; an excellent popular account is given in *The Story of the Bible* by Sir Frederic Kenyon. It is enough here to say that for the next two centuries the efforts of scholars were devoted to the collection and cataloguing of manuscripts, and the amassing of evidence concerning their variant readings. In 1830 a fresh period began, as scholars undertook the sifting of the evidence, the formulation of principles of textual criticism, and the effort to recover the original Greek text, as free as possible from errors and editions. Carl Lachmann opened the period with a revised edition of the Greek text of the New Testament in 1831, which he followed by a larger edition, with fuller evidence, in 1842-50. Then came the epoch-making work of Constantine Tischendorf, discoverer of the Codex Sinaiticus and editor of the Codex Vaticanus, both dating from the fourth century, who published his critical edition of the Greek New Testament with a full textual apparatus in 1869-72. In 1881 after twenty-eight years of joint labor Westcott and Hort, two Cambridge University scholars, published *The New Testament in the Original Greek* in two volumes, the first of which contains the text and the second the introduction and notes. This work presented the oldest and purest Greek text that could be determined in the light of the manuscripts then known. It did not command universal assent, of course, and it must now be supplemented by the results to be drawn from a few notable early manuscripts that have been discovered in the course of the past seventy years; but the work of Westcott and Hort remains, with that of Tischendorf, as a foundation for all subsequent critical study of the Greek text.

The demand for the revision of the King James Version in keeping with the new knowledge of the Greek text acquired strength in the 1850's and 1860's and was met by the action of the Convocation of Canterbury, in May, 1870, authorizing the revision and appointing a Committee to undertake it. Dr. Andrew Edgar in *The Bibles of England* says:

The action taken by that Convocation was not taken a day too soon. So many statements had been scattered abroad, on high authority, that the received version of the Scriptures contains a large number of errors, both in text and translation; and so customary had it become for preachers to tell their hearers that the true text or the true translation, in this and the other passage, is something altogether different from what common people found in their Bibles, that it became necessary for the Church to show her members plainly what the true Bible really is, and what is the total amount of change that modern scholarship alleges should be made on King James's translation.

Westcott and Hort were members of the New Testament Company of the Revision Committee, and confidential advance copies of the Greek text which they were editing were printed for the use of the Revisers in England and America. Though the committee did not always agree with them—there are some two hundred such divergences of judgment—it had full opportunity to avail itself of their research. In all, the committee found that the Greek text underlying the King James Version of the New Testament was erroneous in more than five thousand readings, counting each rejected reading as one, whether it contains one word or several.

With the British committee for the revision of the Bible was associated by correspondence a committee of American scholars organized a year later. The English Revised Version of the New Testament was published in 1881, and that of the Old Testament in 1885. These included only such recommendations of the American committee as were approved by a two-thirds vote of the British committee. The agreement between the two committees was:

If any differences shall still remain, the American Committee will yield its preferences for the sake of harmony; provided that such differences of reading and rendering as the American Committee may represent to the English Companies to be of special importance, be distinctly stated either in the Preface to the Revised Version, or in an Appendix to the volume, during a term of fourteen years from the date of publication, unless the American Churches shall sooner pronounce a deliberate opinion upon the Revised Version with the view of its being taken for public use.

In accordance with this agreement, the American committee prepared an appendix containing by no means a complete list of their recommendations which had been rejected, but a minimum list of those which they deemed to be of sufficient importance to record, in the hope that they might ultimately be incorporated in the text.

After the publication of the Revised Version of the Old Testament in 1885, the British committee disbanded, but the American committee continued its organization, to take such action as should be called for at the expiration of the fourteen-year period. In the meantime, in 1881 and 1882, unauthorized editions of the Revised Version of the New Testament were published in New York and Philadelphia, which incorporated those of the readings preferred by the American committee which had been recorded in the appendix. It is perhaps needless to say that the members of the American committee had not lent their names or their aid to these editions. In 1898 the Oxford and Cambridge University Presses published a similar edition for the American market, with a preface referring to it as the American Revised Bible. These editions were unacceptable to the American committee, since they contained only the preferences included in the appendix, which had purposely been reduced in number. Accordingly, in 1901, the American committee published through Thomas Nelson and Sons *The Holy Bible containing the Old and New Testaments translated out of the original tongues, being the version set forth* A.D. *1611 compared with the most ancient authorities and revised* A.D. *1881-1885. Newly Edited by the American Revision Committee* A.D. *1901.* It was copyrighted "to insure purity of text," and contained on the verso of the title-page the following certification:

This Standard American Edition of the Revised Version of the Bible, and editions in conformity with it published by Messrs. Thomas Nelson and Sons and certified by this endorsement, are the only editions authorized by the American Committee of Revision. George E. Day, Secretary of the Committee, and of the Old Testament Company; J. Henry Thayer, Secretary of the New Testament Company.

This edition contained the full body of the American committee's preferences, and published in an appendix the British readings which they displaced.

I have told this bit of history because it should not be forgotten. The American revision committee was sorely tried in the last two decades of the nineteenth century by those who presumed to do their work for them, without asking for permission, and without seeking to know the full range of their preferences. It was necessary for them to copyright their revision to insure that its text would not be tampered with, and might endure long enough to get a fair trial. And they called it the "Standard" edition because it had to compete with at least three editions that had been mechanically put together by others, and that had usurped the name of "American Version" or "American Revised Bible." The copyright limited the sale, perhaps, and threw them open to misunderstanding; but it protected the integrity of the version, and gave it a chance to live. There was misunderstanding here and there, of course. The editor of the Sunday-school publications of one of the larger denominations told me that when his board adopted the American Standard Version for use in lesson quarterlies and textbooks, he received an indignant letter from one man: "Who is this Tom Nelson who has written a new Bible? I don't want Tom Nelson's Bible. I want the Bible the way the Apostle James wrote it."

The American Standard Version of 1901 has come to be much more widely used in America than the English Revised Version of 1881 and 1885 is used in Great Britain. In 1928 the copyright of this version was transferred to the International Council of Religious Education, and thus it is now owned by the Churches of America which are associated in this Council through their educational boards. The text of the American Standard Version is in charge of the Standard

Bible Committee, a standing committee of scholars appointed by the Council, which is responsible for the integrity of its text, as well as for the work of revision which has now produced the Revised Standard Version. There is no present intention to discontinue its publication, for it well meets the need of those who desire a meticulously exact, literal, word-for-word translation of the Hebrew and Greek.

V

◇◇◇

The Revised Standard Version of the New Testament

THE Revised Standard Version of the New Testament, which was published in 1946, is an authorized revision of the American Standard Version (1901), which is a variant of the English Revised Version (1881), which is a revision of the King James Version (1611).

The authorizing vote of the International Council of Religious Education, acting on behalf of the educational boards of the churches of the United States and Canada which are associated in it, prescribed that the revision should "embody the best results of modern scholarship as to the meaning of the scriptures," and that it should be "designed for use in public and private worship." Further, the Council ordered that the revision should be "in the direction of the simple, classic English style of the King James Version," and that it should "preserve those qualities which have given to the King James Version a supreme place in English literature."

What are these qualities? Surely not the corrupt Greek text upon which the King James Version was based. And surely not the obscurities, the archaisms, and the errors which becloud it. The revisers of 1881 and 1901 corrected many of these. Their work must not be undone. The English Revised Version and the American Standard Version are far more faithful and accurate translations of the Word of God, as found in the Greek New Testament, than the King James Version.

But with all their accuracy, the revised versions of 1881 and 1901 lost some of the beauty and power of the King James Version. This is because they are too obviously "translation English." They are mechanically exact, literal, word-for-word translations which follow the order of the Greek words, so far as this is possible, rather than the order which is natural to English. The present revisers were charged to be no less accurate in translation than their immediate predecessors, but to seek to recover the simplicity, the directness, the literary beauty, and the spiritual power of the King James Version.

The decision to undertake a comprehensive revision of the English Bible was reached only after extended investigation and thorough debate. The American Standard Bible Committee was appointed in 1929, with an original membership of fifteen scholars, to have charge of the text of the American Standard Version, and to make further revision of the text should it be deemed necessary. For more than two years the committee wrestled with the problem of whether or not a revision should be undertaken; and if so, what should be its nature and extent. Representative chapters of the Old Testament and the New Testament were revised by the sections and reported to the committee as a whole; many decisions were made on matters of detail; and the major issue was thoroughly discussed. At the one extreme stood Professor James H. Ropes, who held that the revisions of the King James Version published in 1881 and 1901 ought not to have been made, and opposed any further revision. At the other extreme stood Professor Edgar J. Goodspeed, who advocated a new version in present-day colloquial English. Between these, inclining toward the one side or the other, stood the other members of the committee, with Professor James Moffatt, perhaps, representing the position which finally won general acceptance—that there should be a thorough revision of the version of 1901, which would stay as close to the Tyndale-King James tradition as it could in the light of our present knowledge of the Greek text and its meaning on the one hand, and our present understanding of English on the other.

The Revised Standard Version of the New Testament is not a new translation, in the sense in which Moffatt and Goodspeed have made new translations, without regard to the well-known phrases of the Tyndale-King James tradition. The committee was charged to revise the English New Testament, taking the American Standard Version as a base, and changing it only where it was deemed necessary in the interest of accuracy, clarity, directness, and simplicity. It was instructed to make only such changes in the text as should be agreed upon by a two-thirds vote of the total membership of the committee—a more conservative rule than that which had governed revision in the 1870's, which required only a two-thirds vote of members present.

Yet the Revised Standard Version is in effect a new translation for three reasons. The first is that no adequate revision can be made except upon the basis of as thorough study of the Greek text, and as careful procedure in putting its meaning into English, as would be required in the case of a new translation. The second is that the committee has used the new evidence concerning the Greek text and the new resources for understanding the vocabulary and grammar of the Greek New Testament which have been afforded by the remarkable discoveries of the past sixty years, since the revisions of 1881 and 1901 were made. The third is that the present committee was not obliged, as the former committees were, to maintain the peculiar forms of Elizabethan English in which the King James Version is cast.

It is one of the strange facts of history that the King James Version remained unrevised for two hundred and sixty years, then was revised with the utmost care, but that within less than ten years new evidence began to appear which raised the question of further revision. Instead of 1881 marking the end of a period, Sir Frederic Kenyon says,

a new period was just opening which may rightly be called the Age of Discoveries, since the half-century which has followed since 1881 has seen discovery after discovery widening our knowledge of the Bible text and its early history, and testing the results at which the scholars of 1881 had arrived by evidence with which they were totally unacquainted.[1]

The most important of the manuscripts of portions of the New Testament which have been discovered in this period are the Washington Codex, of the late fourth or the fifth century, and the Chester Beatty Papyri, which date from the early third century. In general, the new evidence as to the Greek text, while of high significance for the development of textual criticism, has not issued in results so different from those reached by the revisers of 1881 and 1901, as to be in itself sufficient reason for a fresh revision of the English text of the New Testament. This evidence affects the scholar's decision as to particular passages, but it does not color the whole of the translation into English.

More pervasive is the new evidence concerning the vocabulary, grammar, and idioms of Hellenistic Greek. That

[1] *The Story of The Bible* (E. P. Dutton & Co.). Copyright 1937 by Sir Frederic Kenyon.

modifies our understanding of Greek usage, and so does color the whole of the translation. An amazing body of Greek papyri has been unearthed in Egypt since the last decade of the nineteenth century—private letters, official reports, wills, business accounts, petitions, and other such trivial, everyday recordings of the ongoing activities of human beings. In 1895 appeared the first of Adolf Deissmann's studies of these commonplace materials. He proved that many words which had hitherto been assumed to belong to what used to be called "biblical Greek" were current in the spoken vernacular of the first century A.D. His discoveries revolutionized the study of New Testament Greek. The New Testament, we now know, was written in the Koine, the common Greek which was spoken and understood practically everywhere throughout the Roman Empire in the early centuries of the Christian era. It was a language without serious differences in dialect; and it covered a larger proportion of the civilized world than English does today. This development in the study of New Testament Greek has come since the work on the English Revised Version and the American Standard Version was done. The revisers were unaware of what was so soon to be learned. The fact that we today bring to the interpretation of New Testament Greek a whole new body of resources developed within the past sixty years makes a revision of the English version of the New Testament imperative.

Complaints about the English of the Revised Version began to be made as soon as it appeared, and they have continued to this day. Charles H. Spurgeon, the great English preacher of the closing nineteenth century, put it tersely when he remarked that the Revised New Testament was "strong in Greek, weak in English." "The Revisers in their scrupulous and conscientious desire to be perfectly true to the Greek have . . . been too unmindful of the claims of their own language," was the comment of Dean Perowne. "They have sometimes been too literal, construing instead of translating; they have inverted the natural order of words in English in order to follow the Greek; and they have carried the translation of the article, and of the tenses, beyond their legitimate limits." A well-balanced and generally favorable article in the *Edinburgh Review* for July, 1881, concluded by saying: "The revisers were not appointed to prepare an interlinear translation for incompetent school-boys." These criticisms, which were made when the English Revised Version was published, apply as well to the American Standard Version. These versions convey the meaning of the Scriptures more accurately than the King James Version, but they have lost some of its directness and vigor.

There were three main reasons for this loss: (1) the principle adopted by the revisers of 1881 and 1901, that they would use the same English word for a given Greek word in every case where it was possible to do this; (2) their precise "interlinear" method of translation; (3) the fact that they were limited to the language of the Elizabethan period or earlier. These reasons will appear as we go on to think of some examples of the problems involved in the choice of the English words and phrases to convey the meaning of the Greek. For convenience and clarity in dealing with a number of variant readings, I shall refer to the several versions by the initial letters of their names, using KJ for the King James Version, ERV for the English Revised Version of 1881, ASV for the American Standard Version of 1901, and RSV for the Revised Standard Version of 1946.

Let us begin with some passages where the King James

Version is in error. In John 10.16 it reads, "And other sheep I have, which are not of this fold: them also I must bring, and they shall hear my voice; and there shall be one fold, and one shepherd." The Greek word for "fold" which is used in the first part of this verse is different from the word used toward the end, which means "flock." Jesus did not say that all of his followers will be in one fold, but that they all belong to his one flock. This verse was correctly translated by Tyndale, but KJ accepted the error from the Bishops' Bible.

The judgment of the Jewish council concerning Jesus (Matt. 26.66) was translated by Tyndale, Cranmer, Geneva, and the Bishops' Bible: "He is worthy to die." But KJ followed the Rhemish Version into an appalling error: "He is guilty of death." The expression is one of the crude Latinisms which so often mar the Rhemish version; and it is hard to understand why the King James translators substituted it for the more correct translation hitherto used. The council did not condemn Jesus as a murderer, guilty of the death of someone. What they said was that he had incurred the penalty of death. RSV translates the sentence: "He deserves to die."

By a strange mistake in prepositions KJ makes Pilate say of Jesus (Luke 23.15): "Nothing worthy of death is done unto him." The revised versions corrected this to read "by him"; RSV, for example, has: "Nothing deserving death has been done by him." A false implication is conveyed by the KJ rendering of Luke 23.32: "And there were also two other malefactors led with him to be put to death." Later printers of the version have sought to guard against the implication that Jesus was a malefactor by using a comma between "other" and "malefactors" and another comma after "malefactors," but that is too weak a device, and likely to fade out in oral reading. ASV reads: "two others, malefactors," which is better, but still weak. RSV gets rid of the implication by rendering the verse: "Two others also, who were criminals, were led away to be put to death with him."

In Matt. 12.14-15 it is reported that the Pharisees took counsel against Jesus, how to destroy him; and KJ goes on to say: "When Jesus knew it, he withdrew." The temporal clause implies that there was a time when Jesus did not know it, an implication that is not justified by the Greek text, which has a simple participle. ASV reads, "Jesus perceiving it . . ."; and RSV has, "Jesus, aware of this."

An error which depends upon a prior error in the Greek text used by KJ, is the phrase "purging all meats" (Mark 7.19). As thus translated it seems to refer to the physical purging of the intestines, whereas the true sense of the passage has to do with the Jewish ceremonial laws concerning food. ASV, adopting the more ancient Greek text, makes the meaning clear by inserting a phrase and translating: "This he said, making all meats clean." RSV puts the sentence in a parenthesis: "(Thus he declared all foods clean.)"

When Herod arrested John the Baptist, KJ tells us that he "observed him" (Mark 6:20), though three of the prior English versions had correctly translated the verb, "kept him." The present revised versions read, "kept him safe."

A mistake that goes back to Tyndale is (Acts 5.30) "whom ye slew and hanged on a tree." ASV translates correctly, "whom ye slew, hanging him on a tree"; and RSV has "whom you killed by hanging him on a tree."

Let us recall the familiar story of Pentecost.

When the day of Pentecost had come, they were all together in one place. And suddenly a sound came from heaven like the rush of a mighty wind, and it filled all the house where they were sitting. And there appeared to them tongues as of fire, distributed and resting on each one of them. And they were all filled with the Holy Spirit and began to speak in other tongues, as the Spirit gave them utterance. (Acts 2.1-4, RSV.)

KJ goes on to say, "Now when this was noised abroad, the multitude came together." That is an utterly misleading statement, implying that the news spread as news will; the correct translation is "when the sound came," that is, the sound from heaven. It was heard by the multitude, not just by those who experienced the gift of the Holy Spirit; and the multitude came together because they had themselves heard the sound, not because they heard a rumor about the sound and its consequences.

A verse which contains both archaisms and errors in translation is Acts 23.27. For convenience, I will italicize the words in question: "This man was *taken of* the Jews, and *should have been* killed *of* them: then *came I* with an *army,* and rescued him, having *understood* that he was a Roman." Here is the archaic use of the preposition "of" in the sense of "by," denoting the actor or agent; here, too, is Tyndale's favorite inversion of subject and predicate. The other italicized words are errors, or at least convey wrong impressions. "Should have been killed" is ambiguous; it was not an "army," but a band of soldiers, that rescued Paul; and the word "understood" gives the impression that the captain knew more of Paul than the Greek indicates that he did. The preceding versions from Tyndale to the Bishops'

Bible had used "soldiers" and "perceiving." RSV translates the verse: "This man was seized by the Jews, and was about to be killed by them, when I came upon them with the soldiers and rescued him, having learned that he was a Roman citizen."

A paradoxical expression is found in Acts 27.21, where Paul says to his shipmates: "Sirs, ye should have hearkened unto me, and not have loosed from Crete, and to have gained this harm and loss." Do people gain loss? Tyndale and Cranmer use the verb "brought"; ASV reads "gotten," and RSV "incurred." The entire sentence, as it stands in KJ, is intolerably loose. In RSV it reads: "Men, you should have listened to me, and should not have set sail from Crete and incurred this injury and loss." A few verses further on (Acts 27.40) KJ reads, "When they had taken up the anchors, they committed themselves unto the sea"—a statement which is untrue if it is taken that they jumped overboard, and is meaningless otherwise. The revised versions agree on the meaning expressed in RSV: "They cast off the anchors, and left them in the sea."

In 1 Tim. 6.5 KJ follows all other sixteenth-century versions except Coverdale in mistaking the predicate for the subject: "supposing that gain is godliness." The revised versions correct this mistake, and the clause appears in RSV: "imagining that godliness is a means of gain."

Paul's injunction to the Thessalonians is not, "Abstain from all appearance of evil," as KJ puts it, but "Abstain from every form of evil" (1 Thess. 5.22). To the Galatians (6.11) his word is not, "Ye see how large a letter I have written unto you with mine own hand," but, "See with what large letters I am writing to you with my own hand." KJ causes

Paul to make a strange claim of sinlessness in 2 Cor. 5:21: "For he hath made him to be sin for us, who knew no sin." But Paul said nothing that can be translated "for us, who knew no sin." ASV renders this text: "Him who knew no sin he made to be sin on our behalf." RSV has: "For our sake he made him to be sin who knew no sin."

"He that giveth, let him do it with simplicity" (Rom. 12.8) is an oddly misleading exhortation, in view of the fact that the word here represented by "simplicity" means, and is in similar contexts of the KJ translated, "liberality." Even more misleading is the KJ translation of 2 Cor. 11.3: "But I fear lest . . . your minds should be corrupted from the simplicity that is in Christ." ASV, using a somewhat different Greek text, renders it "the simplicity and the purity that is toward Christ," which is a strangely puzzling expression. RSV translates the verse: "But I am afraid that . . . your thoughts will be led astray from a sincere and pure devotion to Christ."

In 1 Cor. 1.21 a phrase appears that is often quoted, and is so misleading that it should be eradicated from our thought and speech. That phrase is "the foolishness of preaching"—"It pleased God by the foolishness of preaching to save them that believe." Earlier also, in verse 18, the KJ translators gave a wrong twist to the meaning, saying that "the preaching of the cross is to them that perish foolishness," whereas the Greek has "the word of the cross." It was not preaching as a method of conveying the message of the Cross that seemed to be foolish; it was the content of the message itself. It is the gospel, the good news of what God did in Christ for the salvation of men that seems to be folly to the minds of those who are unable or unwilling to discern its wisdom. RSV translates verse 18: "For the word of the cross is folly to those who are perishing, but to us who are being saved it is the power of God"; and verse 21: "For since, in the wisdom of God, the world did not know God through wisdom, it pleased God through the folly of what we preach to save those who believe."

The printers of the King James Version have not been consistent in their modernization of spelling. For example, "cloke" remains for "cloak"; and "throughly" is kept in Luke 3.17 as the spelling for "thoroughly." "Lift" is retained as the past tense in Luke 16.23, but it is changed to "lifted" in Luke 11.27 and elsewhere. "Broided" is the old form of "braided," and in 1 Tim. 2.9 women are still advised not to adorn themselves with "broided hair." As early as 1633, a printer changed the word, either purposely or by inadvertence, to "broidered," and this misprint was handed on for many years, though it has now disappeared. The revised versions use "braided." Another printer's change in the same verse has unfortunately remained. The KJ translators wrote, "that women adorn themselves in modest apparel, with shamefastness and sobriety," and so the text appeared in 1611 and for fifty years thereafter. Then, through some printer's error, the word "shamefacedness" appeared, and it has been kept to this day. That is entirely unfair to the translators, for the word which they used, "shamefastness," referred to character, while "shamefacedness" refers to appearance. Paul may be accused of failing to afford to women their full and proper place, but at least he did not exhort them to go about shamefacedly. RSV translates this text: "that women should adorn themselves modestly and sensibly in seemly apparel."

As published in 1611, KJ consistently used the phrase "such a one," but in time the printers changed this to "such an one," except in 2 Cor. 2.7, where the original phrase remains. There is no good excuse for "such an one," which is hard to pronounce and not in accord with good English usage.

Another group of expressions which call for revision consists of cases in which different forms of the same English word are used indiscriminately. Thus the King James Version of the New Testament uses both "afore" and "before," "aforehand" and "beforehand," "aforetime" and "beforetime," "afterward" and "afterwards," "alway" and "always," "in time past" and "in times past," "in old time" and "in the old time." It uses "whiles" as well as "while." "Sometime" and "sometimes" have distinct meanings now, "sometime" referring to some particular date or period in the past or future, while "sometimes" means "occasionally." KJ uses the two words without distinction, and always in the sense of reference to past time. This is almost sure to be misunderstood by the modern reader, who will think that when Paul writes "ye who sometimes were far off" (Eph. 2.13) and "we ourselves also were sometimes foolish" (Tit. 3.3), he is referring to merely occasional remoteness or folly.

The verb "stablish" is used eight times and "establish" eleven times, with the same meaning, as can readily be seen by comparing Rom. 1.11 and 16.25. "Ensample" is used six times and "example" eight times. A light from heaven "shined" about Paul on the road to Damascus (Acts 9.3), but in his address to the people at Jerusalem he says that it "shone." Writing to the Corinthians (2 Cor. 4.6), Paul says that "God hath shined in our hearts"; but in Luke's account of the shepherds in the field by night, "the glory of the Lord shone round about them."

The words "specially" and "especially" are used indiscriminately, in translation of the same Greek word, and always in the meaning of "especially." For example, in Acts 25.26, Paul is brought "specially" before King Agrippa, and in 26.3 he is "especially" happy that this opportunity to be heard is afforded him. Both "ware" and "aware" are used in the same sense (compare Acts 14.6 with Luke 11.44; 12.46). The verb "beware" is used in a number of places, and is once split open to read "be thou ware" (2 Tim. 4.15). In Matt. 7.28 "the people were astonished at his doctrine"; and in Mark 11.18 "the people was astonished at his doctrine." Ananias "gave up the ghost" and Sapphira "yielded up the ghost"; but in the Greek they did exactly the same thing (Acts 5.5, 10).

Paul reminds the Thessalonians "what manner of men we were among you for your sake" (1 Thess. 1.5), but a little further on in the same letter (3.9) refers to "the joy wherewith we joy for your sakes." With all their care to be consistent the revisers of 1881 and 1901 failed to correct this lapse. The Greek is identical; and the latter of the two forms is indefensible, for the expression translates a prepositional phrase. We would not say "for the sakes of you," even if the "you" were plural.

Before words beginning with a vowel KJ generally uses the possessive "mine," as "mine eyes," "mine enemies"; but we also find the word "my" in similar positions, as "my oxen" (Matt. 22.4) and "my affairs" (Eph. 6.21). The word "none" is generally used by KJ before words beginning with a vowel, as "none other," "none occasion"; but it also has "no other" (1 Tim. 1.3), and "no evil" (2 Cor. 13.7).

The King James Version inherited much of Tyndale's lack of care for consistency. Matt. 26.41 and Mark 14.38 are identical in the Greek; but Matthew reads, "Watch and pray, that ye enter not into temptation; the spirit indeed is willing, but the flesh is weak"; and Mark, "Watch ye and pray, lest ye enter into temptation. The spirit truly is ready, but the flesh is weak." The statement in Gen. 15.6 concerning Abraham's faith is quoted three times in the New Testament: "it was counted unto him for righteousness" (Rom. 4.3); "it was accounted to him for righteousness" (Gal. 3.6); "it was imputed unto him for righteousness" (James 2.23). In Tyndale's quotations of this statement, the three verbs were "counted," "ascribed," "reputed."

There are many instances in KJ of obsolete or inaccurate usage of pronouns, adverbs, prepositions, and conjunctions. The preposition "of" is constantly used where we would now say "by"—Jesus is said to be baptized of John, and led of the spirit into the wilderness to be tempted of the devil. It is used in the place of "for"—Herod desired to see Jesus "of a long season" (Luke 23.8), and "of long time" Simon had bewitched the people of Samaria. "The zeal of thine house" means "zeal for thy house" (John 2.17), and "a zeal of God" means "zeal for God" (Rom. 10.2). "Of" is also used for "from"—in Mark 9.21, the father's answer to the question how long his son had been afflicted with a dumb spirit is translated "Of a child," and means "From childhood."

"To" is sometimes used by KJ in the sense of "for"—"We have Abraham to our father" (Luke 3.8). It is used for "with" in the expression "to him they agreed" (Acts 5.40); and it is simply in the way when Paul is made to say "his servants ye are to whom ye obey" (Rom. 6.16). RSV renders the latter passage: "You are slaves of the one whom you obey."

Paul's statement in 1 Cor. 4.4, "I know nothing by myself," means "I know nothing against myself." The preposition "by" was also used by KJ in the sense of "during" or "for" as part of the phrase "by the space of"—"This continued by the space of two years" (Acts 19.10). It is one of the odd facts about the King James Version of the New Testament that whenever it uses the word "space" it refers to a period of time.

The preposition "without" is used in the sense of "beyond" in one of the less comprehensible verses of the King James Version (2 Cor. 10.13): "We will not boast of things without our measure, but according to the measure of the rule which God hath distributed to us, a measure to reach even unto you." ASV clears the meaning of the first clause by using "beyond," but gets into further trouble by bringing in the word "province": "We will not glory beyond our measure, but according to the measure of the province which God apportioned to us as a measure, to reach even unto you." RSV translates it: "We will not boast beyond limit but will keep to the limits God has apportioned us, to reach even to you."

The term "by and by" in KJ means "immediately." Unless we know this, the verse describing the request of the daughter of Herodias seems oddly inconsistent (Mark 6.25): "She came in straightway with haste unto the king, and asked, saying, I will that thou give me by and by in a charger the head of John the Baptist." The words "presently" and "anon" also mean "immediately." The word "instantly," however, does not have a temporal meaning in KJ; it is used in the sense of "urgently." The word "constantly" in KJ means "consistently" or "firmly," that is, "with constancy," and is so used of the maid Rhoda, who recognized Peter's voice, and "constantly affirmed that it was even so" (Acts 12.15).

There is some bad grammar in the King James Version. Much of it is failure to observe agreement in singular or plural number, the rule for which was very loosely observed in the century when our English translations of the Bible were being made. In Luke 9.17 we read that "there was taken up . . . twelve baskets." When Simon Peter was astonished at the miraculous draught of fish that he had taken at the Master's command, the account goes on: "And so was also James and John, . . . which were partners with Simon" (Luke 5.10). Jesus is reported as saying (Luke 11.29): "This is an evil generation; they seek a sign, and there shall no sign be given it." The chief priests and Pharisees, seeking Jesus, commanded "that if any man knew where he were, he should shew it" (John 11.57).

In Matt. 18.12 the question about the man who has lost a sheep reads: "doth he not leave the ninety and nine and goeth . . . ?" but in Luke 15.4 the same question is put correctly: "What man of you . . . doth not leave the ninety and nine and go . . . ?" A mixture of subjunctive and indicative modes appears in John 9.31: "if any man be a worshipper of God, and doeth his will." ASV made both verbs subjunctive: "be . . . and do." RSV makes both indicative: "if any one is a worshiper of God and does his will." Mark 8.22 reads: "they bring a blind man unto him, and besought him to touch him." In the Greek both verbs are in the present tense, and ASV so translates: "bring . . . and beseech." RSV regards both as historical presents, and reads, "brought to him a blind man, and begged him to touch him." In Luke 23.8 we read that when Herod saw Jesus, "he hoped to have seen some miracle done by him." It is an error that goes back to Tyndale; the Greek reads, and good English demands, "to see"—"he hoped to see some miracle done by him."

Indefinite pronouns, referring to any person, use the masculine forms in the Greek, just as we in English often use the pronoun "he" in a general statement including both sexes. The King James Version overdoes this masculine habit by its general use of "no man" and "any man" where the meaning is "no one" or "any one." This practice limits many statements unduly, and results in occasional infelicities. In Matt. 11.27 it is said that "No man knoweth the Son, but the Father." The word "but" is ambiguous here, for it may mean that men do not know the Son but do know the Father. That is absurd, but if the meaning is "no man knoweth the Son, except the Father," it involves a worse absurdity by implying that the Father is a man. The Greek is perfectly clear, and ASV clearly translates it: "No one knoweth the Son, save the Father." RSV has: "No one knows the Son except the Father."

The major problem with respect to the King James Version is, of course, its archaic language. You will recall how strikingly that problem is put in the statement by the Church of Scotland:

The Authorised Version is becoming unable to fulfill the function it was created to serve, because the language in which it is written is not the language our people speak, or readily understand, today. . . . Many words and phrases which were current coin in 1611 have fallen out of circulation; many words have changed their meanings, some have appreciated in value, others have depreciated, some have acquired a broader meaning, others a narrower; the general manner of using the language, the style, and even the syntax have changed. The consequence is that to those of our people, especially of the younger generation, who have not had more than an elementary schooling in language and literature, there is a great deal in the Authorised Version which is simply incomprehensible. . . . There is the further danger that even where the language of the Bible is intelligible, the archaic flavour may well give the impression that the message of the Bible itself belongs to a bygone age and has no relevance to the world of the twentieth century.

We face two distinct problems with respect to the archaic language of the King James Version. The first of these is concerned with particular words that have changed in meaning, and have therefore become misleading. The second is concerned with the general style and atmosphere of the version, with its air of belonging to the history of English literature but becoming increasingly irrelevant to life and even to worship.

Webster defines the adjective "archaic," as applied to language, thus: "Obsolete in ordinary language but retained in special context or for special uses; as, (a) in Biblical, ecclesiastical, and legal expressions; (b) in poetry or narrative, to suggest associations with olden times or to simulate the language of a former period."

Now the fact is that the really obsolete words of the King James Version of the New Testament—the words that are no longer used in current language—do not present much of a problem. There are not many such words, and their meaning can be guessed from the context, if one chances not to know it. Among them are "dure" (Matt. 13.21), "hoise" (Acts 27.40), "trow" (Luke 17.9), and "wit," "wist," and "wot." The only example of the use of any of these obsolete words that can perplex any ordinarily sensible reader is (2 Cor. 8.1): "we do you to wit of the grace of God," which means "we make known to you."

The words that cause trouble are those which are not obsolete but have acquired a different meaning from that which they had for the King James translators. It is not because the word "let" is obsolete that it is no longer suitable for use in Rom. 1.13, "I purposed to come unto you, but was let hitherto"; it is because the word has lost the meaning of "hindered" or "restrained," and has acquired precisely the opposite meaning. If the word "prevent" were obsolete, the ordinary reader might fail to guess at its meaning in 1 Thess. 4.15, "we which are alive and remain unto the coming of the Lord shall not prevent them which are asleep"; but he would not attribute to it a totally wrong meaning. In 1611 the word "prevent" meant "go before," "precede" or "anticipate"; it now means to hinder, restrain, or render impossible.

There are about two hundred English words and phrases which were used in the King James Version in a sense that they no longer convey to the reader. Some of them have completely lost the sense in which they were then used; others may retain this sense for the expert in language, but have acquired other meanings or associations which displace it in current usage. We are on safe ground if we maintain that no word should be kept in the English version of the New Testament that has acquired a connotation that is misleading. The question which the reviser must raise in each case is not so much whether the word has entirely lost the meaning it once had, but whether it has picked up new meanings which so deflect or reshape it as to impair its fitness to express in English the meaning of the Greek text.

A typical word is "suffer." The King James translators used it in the sense of let, allow, permit, as well as in its primary sense of endure or undergo. It still has the meaning "let," but this is so overlaid with the basic idea of enduring hardship, pain, affliction, insult, penalty, and the like, that no one would think today of using the verb "suffer" when all that he means to say is a simple, straightforward "let."

It chances that I had an interesting experience with this word. In the summer of 1946, a few months after the Revised Standard Version of the New Testament had been published, I received a letter from an old friend, a minister well up in years, who expressed approval of the new version, but said: "I cannot help regretting that the children who read it will no longer have that precious spiritual possession, 'Suffer little children to come unto me, and forbid them not: for of such is the kingdom of God.'" Within a day or two after receiving this letter I went by plane to London, and there was asked to speak to a group of teachers and church leaders concerning the Revised Standard Version. In the subsequent discussion, the first question was by a woman who is engaged in the religious education of children in the Church of England: "What does the RSV do with the text, 'Suffer little children to come unto me'?"

I answered, "It reads: 'Let the children come to me, and do not hinder them; for to such belongs the kingdom of God.'"

She said, "Well, I am thankful that at last we have that text put into words that children can understand."

The word "conversation" in KJ means "conduct" or "manner of life"; and the word "communicate" was used in the sense of "share." To "comfort" meant to strengthen and inspire, rather than simply to console or soothe. "Virtue" was used in the sense of "power." "Bowels" was used for "affection" or "kindness," being a literal translation of the Greek, where the intestines stood for the seat of the affections, just as the heart does in English. It is not to the credit of the KJ that it followed the Rhemish version in a literal translation of this word in every case, when Tyndale, the Great Bible, and the Genevan Bible had in some of its occurrences used "compassion" or "tender mercy." "Record" was used in the sense of "witness." Phil. 1.8 reads in KJ: "For God is my record, how greatly I long after you all in the bowels of Jesus Christ." RSV renders this: "For God is my witness, how I yearn for you all with the affection of Christ Jesus."

"Worship" was used in KJ in the sense of the respect or honor due to superior rank or merit. Recall Jesus' saying (Luke 14.10): "When he that bade thee cometh, he may say unto thee, Friend, go up higher: then shalt thou have worship in the presence of them that set at meat with thee." We cannot today use the word worship in many of the contexts where it is used by KJ.

It must be confusing for children and young people of today, who are being told that respect for persons is a basic principle of sound democracy and true religion, to read in the Bible that "God is no respecter of persons" (Acts 10.34). But the word "person," in the sixteenth century, was still close to its derivation from the Latin *persona,* the mask that an actor wore. It referred to the outward circumstances or external appearance of men, rather than to intrinsic worth or to the inner springs of conscious self-determining being. This text and others using similar words mean simply that

God does not regard mere externals. Tyndale and Geneva translated it, "God is not partial." RSV has, "God shows no partiality."

There are a number of words that were employed in King James's time in a good or at least harmless sense, which have now acquired worse or more violent meanings. "Base" simply meant "lowly" or "humble"—"I, Paul, who in presence am base among you" (2 Cor. 10.1). "Vile" was no worse—"our vile body" (Phil. 3.21) is rendered by RSV, "our lowly body"; and the poor man's "vile raiment" (James 2.2) is "shabby clothing." The word "provoke" meant simply "call forth." "I know the forwardness of your mind, . . . " KJ has Paul write to the Corinthians, "and your zeal hath provoked very many" (2 Cor. 9.2). But the "forwardness" was simply "readiness," and the provoking was not to anger, but to emulation in generosity. When we read concerning John the Baptist that "the soldiers demanded of him, saying, And what shall we do?" (Luke 3.14), we get an impression of peremptoriness that did not belong to the word "demand" in 1611, when it simply meant "ask." "Riot" and "rioting" referred then to revelry and loose living rather than to turbulence and violence. "Addicted" was then employed in a good sense but now is generally used of bad habits. The KJ rendering "they have addicted themselves to the ministry of the saints" has been changed in RSV to read, "they have devoted themselves to the service of the saints" (1 Cor. 16.15). The word "unspeakable" tends to be applied now to bad rather than to good things; RSV therefore has "Thanks be to God for his inexpressible gift!" (2 Cor. 9.15), and "rejoice with unutterable joy" (1 Pet. 1.8).

These are but a few—only sixteen—of about two hundred English words and phrases which were used in the King

James version in a sense substantially different from that which they now convey. They were then accurate translations of the Greek; they have now become misleading. It not only does the King James translators no honor, but it is quite unfair to them, to retain these words which now convey a meaning that they did not intend.

VI

The Use of the New Testament
in Worship

WHEN the Revised Standard Version of the New Testament appeared in 1946, a few newspaper columnists commented upon what they supposed to be the futility of revising the King James Version. "Who would think," they said, "of revising Shakespeare?" Who, indeed? The fact that they made this comparison simply shows how little they understand the importance of the Bible or its relevance to life.

The message of the Bible is the central thing, its style is but an instrument for conveying the message. The Bible is not a mere historical document to be preserved. And it is more than a classic of English literature to be cherished and admired. The Bible contains the Word of God to man. And men need the Word of God in our time and hereafter as never before. That Word must not be disguised in phrases that are no longer clear, or hidden under words that have changed or lost their meaning. It must stand forth in language that is direct and plain and meaningful to people today.

The committee was instructed to prepare a Revised Standard Version which would not only present the meaning of the Scriptures clearly in the light of modern scholarship but would also be designed for use in public and private worship. Both of these aims have been before it constantly.

At one meeting, when a proffered reading of the up-to-date type was rejected by a decisive vote, its propounder addressed Dr. Moffatt: "Do you know where I got that phrase?"

"No," was the answer.

"I got it from Moffatt's *New Translation*."

Dr. Moffatt replied without hesitation: "That was all right for my translation; but it will not do for this. We are making this translation for use in public worship in the churches."

Nevertheless, a few months after the Revised Standard Version of the New Testament had been published I met an old friend, a well-known Christian layman, who warmly expressed his interest in it, saying that he had read straight through it as he would any other book and that he had found much new light on the meaning of the New Testament, especially in the epistles of Paul. When I asked him whether his minister read from it in public worship, he looked at me with sudden suspicion. "Do you mean that it is intended to be read from the pulpit?" When I answered that it is intended for that very purpose as well as for teaching and private reading he was polite and noncommittal; but I got the impression that he was unconvinced.

In the end, the crucial test of the Revised Standard Version of the New Testament will be in worship. If men, women, and children are led by it to God, and if they find its phrases naturally upon their lips and in their hearts when they pray, it will endure. If ministers and people find in it the Word of God, as it is read in the services of the church and expounded in preaching, it will live and bring newness of life to many. If not, the attempt to revise the King James Version will have to be made again. One thing is sure: the

English-speaking world will not always be content with a version as faulty as the King James is now seen to be. If it should appear that the present committee has failed, some other company of revisers will in due time succeed.

Much of what is said as to the value of the King James Version for use in worship is without any sound basis. One man argued that we should always say, "Our Father which art in heaven" because the word "which" removes God from the company of men, and sets him apart as unique and transcendent. The King James translators would have laughed at such an interpretation; for them the relative pronoun "which" had the meaning that the relative pronoun "who" now has. Another argued that the ungrammatical "whom" in Jesus' question at Caesarea Philippi is more musical and thus more worshipful than the word "who" can be.

Paul's defense before the people of Jerusalem begins: "I am a Jew, born at Tarsus in Cilicia . . . " The first four words are a perfectly natural translation—in fact the only natural translation into English—of the Greek. The careful, literal-minded revisers of 1881 and 1901 led the way for those of 1946 on that point. Yet after a recent lecture, a man came forward who stoutly defended the expression here used by the King James Version, "I am verily a man which am a Jew." He said that this is more euphonious, more rhythmical, and stronger than the simple statement; and that therefore it ought to be retained in any version of the New Testament designed for use in public worship. How is one to deal with assertions like that? The Greek contains no word for "verily" and no word for "which am." Anyone who imagines that Paul would stammer about with the Hebrew or Aramaic equivalent of "I am verily a man which am a Jew" as the first statement in his supreme opportunity to proclaim the gospel to the people of Jerusalem has not learned to know Paul. And anyone who sees strength and euphony in this dwells in a universe of values appropriate to a Gilbert and Sullivan comic opera.

The discouraging feature of this last case is that the man is a college professor and yet assumed that the present translation, "I am a Jew," is an innovation. He did not know that it had been so rendered by the revisers of the 1870's; indeed, he seemed to know only by vague hearsay that the English Revised Version and the American Standard Version exist. His mind was set upon one idea, that the King James Version is suited to use in public worship and that no revision of it ever can be. He was typical of the people for whom the question is settled by habit and familiarity, and who are not interested enough to give any revised version a fair trial. One man protested vigorously against the use of any other than the King James Version in public worship on the ground that "changes of phraseology make me think, and I don't want to think when I worship."

Are thought and worship incompatible? Must we use two translations of the Scriptures into English, one for the mind and another for the heart? It may be that no version of the New Testament which states its meaning clearly will arouse as much of "the feeling of the numinous" as one that is more obscure. And it is possible, of course, that in seeking to be clear the makers of the Revised Standard Version have only succeeded in being commonplace. Time will tell. I venture to believe that neither of these sentences is true.

The English Revised Version and its variant, the American Standard Version, were not only based upon a more accurate Greek text than the King James Version, they also cleared up many of its English inconsistencies and obscurities. But the revisers' method of doing this was too labored and precise. What was needed was not so much a clarity that would emerge when carefully studied, as a clarity that shines out immediately. This they did not attain. On the contrary, they lost some of the directness which the King James Version had. That was because of their word-for-word method of translating, using the same English word for a given Greek word whenever possible, leaving no Greek word without translation into a correspondent English word, following the order of the Greek words rather than the order natural to English, and attempting to translate the articles and the tenses with a precision alien to English idioms. The Greek particle *oun*, for example, is too often overtranslated in these versions as "therefore," and *kai* as "also"—both "therefore" and "also" being words that are less frequently used in English, and consequently loom larger when they are used, than *oun* and *kai* in the Greek New Testament. The disposition to follow the Greek word order led to such unnecessary changes as "Thy will be done, as in heaven, so on earth," and such awkward English as "They ate and were all filled; and there was taken up that which remained over to them of broken pieces, twelve baskets" (Luke 9.17). Another example is John 17.1-2, which reads in KJ: "Glorify thy Son, that thy Son also may glorify thee; as thou hast given him power over all flesh, that he should give eternal life to as many as thou hast given him." ERV complicates the reading thus: "Glorify thy Son, that the Son may glorify thee; even as thou gavest him authority over all flesh, that whatsoever thou hast given him, to them he should give eternal life." ASV is a bit simpler, changing the last clause to read: "that to all whom thou hast given him, he should give eternal life." RSV returns to the more natural English order:

"Glorify thy Son that the Son may glorify thee, since thou hast given him power over all flesh, so that he might give eternal life to all whom thou hast given him."

For an example of overprecision in use of the definite article, let me quote the comment of Dr. Andrew Edgar:

One verse that has been much lauded by scholastic admirers for its precision of statement, but which, from the frequent iteration of the definite article, strains and perplexes the untutored intellect of the common reader and throws him into acrobatic attitudes of imagination which are too much for him, is Romans 5.15: "Not as *the* trespass so also is *the* free gift. For if by *the* trespass of *the* one *the* many died, much more did *the* grace of God, and *the* gift by *the* grace of *the* one man, Jesus Christ, abound unto *the* many."

That verse contains ten occurrences of the article "the"; KJ has five. RSV keeps five, and gives a clearer translation: "But the free gift is not like the trespass. For if many died through one man's trespass, much more have the grace of God and the free gift in the grace of that one man Jesus Christ abounded for many."

For the tenses, let me again quote a comment by Dr. Edgar:

In their zeal to present literally the exact significance of every tense in the Greek verb, the revisers have occasionally introduced forms of expression that are little better than conundrums. We have been accustomed to read in Hebrews 11.5: "before his translation he (Enoch) had this testimony that he pleased God." This plain and easily comprehended statement has been changed by the revisers into the following grammatical and historical puzzle: "before his translation he *hath had* witness borne to him that he *had* been well pleasing unto God."

This comment is on ERV; it is even more deserved by ASV, which further complicates the verse by a change of order: "He hath had witness borne to him that before his translation he had been well-pleasing to God." RSV returns to a simpler statement: "Before he was taken he was attested as having pleased God."

In the course of the two years of experiment and debate which led to the decision to undertake a new revision, the Standard Bible Committee was led to the conclusion, from which only one member dissented, that the generally archaic style of the English translation of the New Testament should no longer be maintained.

The revisers in the 1870's were bound by their instructions to adhere to this generally archaic style. This is what they say about the limitations under which they worked:

The second of the rules, by which the work has been governed, prescribed that the alterations to be introduced should be expressed, as far as possible, in the language of the Authorized Version or of the Versions that preceded it. To this rule we have faithfully adhered. We have habitually consulted the earlier Versions; and in our sparing introduction of words not found in them or in the Authorized Version we have usually satisfied ourselves that such words were employed by standard writers of nearly the same date, and had also that general hue which justified their introduction into a Version which has held the highest place in the classical literature of our language. We have never removed any archaisms, whether in structure or in words, except where we were persuaded either that the meaning of the words was not generally understood, or that the nature of the expression led to some misconception of the true sense of the passage. The frequent inversions of the strict order of the words, which add much to the strength and variety of the Authorized Version, and give an archaic colour to many felicities of diction, have been seldom modified. Indeed, we have often adopted the same arrangement in our own alterations; and in this, as in other particulars, we have sought to assimilate the new work to the old.

The American committee, in preparing the American Standard Version of 1901, went further in the removal of particular archaisms—for example, they substituted "Holy Spirit" for "Holy Ghost," "once" for "aforetime," "hungry" for "an hungred," and so on. The list of the differences between ERV and ASV is given in the appendix to any of the larger editions of the latter. It is not completely given in the appendix to the ERV, for reasons earlier explained.

Whether in the form of ERV or ASV, the revision authorized in 1870 was limited in the vocabulary it could use and was driven toward artificiality by the requirement that it move within the language and usage of the sixteenth century. One result of this limitation, together with the further attempt of the revisers to represent every Greek word and particle by a corresponding English word, is that the revised versions are sometimes more archaic than the King James Version. At various points the revisers introduced archaisms. They greatly, and unnecessarily, increased the use of such words as "howbeit," "holden," "aforetime," "sojourn," "must needs," "would fain," and "behooved." They joined the word "haply" to the word "lest" in seventeen cases where KJ did not have it; the RSV has eliminated the word "haply" in all cases. An example of inserted archaism that seems almost ridiculous is in 1 Thess. 5.18, where KJ read "This is the will of God in Christ Jesus concerning you." ERV and ASV changed this to read, "This is the will of God in Christ Jesus to you-ward." No proper reason can be assigned for this. It was not required by the revisers' own practice; they had used the preposition "toward" three times in verses 14 and 15. It was not a general practice of the King James Version, in which the word "toward" is used some fifty times, "to God-ward" twice, and "to you-ward" and "to us-ward" once each. It was not suggested by Tyndale, for he had "toward you" in this verse. It looks as though the revisers simply decided that here was a good place to add some archaic color. RSV reads, "This is the will of God in Christ Jesus for you."

The comparison of the King James Version and the American Standard Version with one another, and the study of both in the light of our present knowledge of the Greek text and its meaning, led the committee to the conclusion that the limitation to sixteenth-century language and usage imposed upon the revisers of 1881 and 1901 a problem that is artificial and admits of no satisfactory solution. Further, the generally archaic style of the King James Version has now become a hindrance to worship as well as to understanding.

It is not the archaisms of the King James Version that have given to it a supreme place in English literature. Archaisms are forms of expression that grow old and pass out of use. They are "the things that are shaken," so that "those things which cannot be shaken may remain." The beauty and power of the King James Version lie in something deeper than archaic forms of speech and writing; they lie in the basic structure which this version inherited from William Tyndale. Recall what we have said about Tyndale's translation of the New Testament—that it was more definite and concise than the style current in his day; that it is simple, clear

English prose, disciplined by his high conception of his task; that it is remarkably compendious, to use Tyndale's term, or terse and compact, as we would say today. These are general terms, and if an author had nothing of importance to say, he might be as simple, clear, concise, and disciplined as one could wish yet be trivial and dull. But if the content of the ideas is significant and if fact and imagination be present, these qualities help to make great literature.

The vocabulary and idioms of the English New Testament ought not to be dated. It was a mistake in the 1870's to limit revision to the vocabulary and idioms of the sixteenth century; it had been a greater mistake for Harwood to clothe it in the pomposity of the eighteenth century and for Dickinson to try to adorn it with the "splendid and sweetly flowing diction" of the early nineteenth. So, too, it would now be a mistake to limit the revision to the language of today, the vocabulary and idioms characteristic of the middle twentieth century. One enthusiastic inquirer raised the question whether we have made Paul speak in terms of "the atomic era." To this the answer is an emphatic "No." The committee sought to put the message of the New Testament in simple, enduring words that are worthy to stand in the great tradition of Tyndale and the King James Version, purged of its archaisms and made clear in meaning. They tried to use relatively timeless words and idioms, instead of those that are merely the language of our time. And they kept to the basic structure of the tradition, conscious that their work is that of revisers, and seeking to maintain its disciplined freedom and compactness.

The Revised Standard Version retains the second person singular, "thou," with its correlative forms, "thee," "thy," "thine," and the verb endings "-est" and "-edst," only in the language of prayer, addressed to God. The "-eth and "-th" forms for verb endings in the third person are not used at all. Something is lost, be it granted, by the elimination of the plural nominative "ye"; but this is a loss that has been sustained by the English language.

"Is come" means "has come," and in general "is," "are," and other forms of the verb "be" as auxiliaries for the perfect tense of intransitive verbs of motion, are replaced by the corresponding forms of the verb "have."

In general, the Revised Standard Version uses the simpler forms. "To" is used instead of "unto," and usually "on" replaces "upon." "Enter into" is "enter." (ASV in one verse, John 18.15, has "entered in . . . into.") The "so" is omitted from "whosoever," "whatsoever," and the like. "According as" is simply "as." "Insomuch that" is "so that." "They that" and "them that" are "those who." "Because that" and "for that" are "because" and "for." "Was yet a coming" and "I go a fishing" lose their "a." "The more part" is "the majority." "Nothing bettered" is "no better." "Compass round" is "surround." "Exceeding" and "sore" are not used as adverbs. Such expressions as "on this wise," "set at naught," "the which," "an eight days," and "on sleep," and such words as "privily," "wherein," "whereby," "thereabout," and "divers" are replaced by modern equivalents. In the use of "shall" and "will" modern usage is followed.

The effect of changes such as these may be indicated by the quotation of a few verses. In Luke 20.20 the description of the spies in KJ, "which should feign themselves just men," became in ASV, "who feigned themselves to be righteous," and now reads in RSV, "who pretended to be sincere." In 2 Cor. 10.6 KJ has bad English: "having in a readiness to revenge all disobedience." ASV changes to "being in readiness to avenge all disobedience"; and RSV has "being ready to punish every disobedience." The renderings of Rom. 1.28 are: KJ, "Even as they did not like to retain God in their knowledge, God gave them over to a reprobate mind, to do those things which are not convenient"; ASV, "Even as they refused to have God in their knowledge, God gave them up unto a reprobate mind, to do those things which are not fitting"; RSV, "since they did not see fit to acknowledge God, God gave them up to a base mind and to improper conduct." The renderings of Phil. 4.14 are: KJ, "Notwithstanding ye have well done, that ye did communicate with my affliction"; ASV, "Howbeit ye did well that ye had fellowship with my affliction"; RSV, "Yet it was kind of you to share my trouble."

The style of the Revised Standard Version is direct. The inverted order of subject and predicate is avoided except where it seems necessary to convey the emphasis of the Greek. The number of suspended clauses is reduced to that minimum which the Greek demands. The aim has been to present a version easy to read aloud in public worship, and not hard for hearers to understand. The clauses are therefore put in a natural order, and the sentences are sometimes shorter than in the versions of 1611 and 1881-1901. Care has been given to rhythm, euphony, and cadences.

The revisers purposely kept as much as possible of the time-honored phrases in those passages of the New Testament which are most constantly used in public worship, such as the Lord's Prayer, the Magnificat, and the Benedictus. Probably the truest test of the value of the Revised Standard Version is not to be found in these passages, or in other great passages with which people are most familiar, such as the Christmas story, the Easter message, Paul's account of the institution of the Lord's supper, the portrait of love in 1 Cor. 13, the psalm of faith in Heb. 11, and the like. When people read the passages they know best, they are apt to think that they know more than they do, and to be unduly disturbed by any change. Test the version in these passages, by all means; it will stand the testing. But it is more important to test it also by reading relatively unfamiliar passages, which have hitherto had no special meaning or value for you. If these unfamiliar passages begin to interest you, as you read them in the new version, it will be successful. For its aim is to clear up the obscurities and correct the errors which have marred the King James Version, particularly in the translation of the epistles.

Many times during the years that the revisers were at work upon this version of the New Testament they were asked to release sections of the text for publication in various news stories. They refused all such requests, partly because the work was unfinished, and partly because they did not wish the public to form judgments concerning the Revised Standard Version upon a basis of fragments, without opportunity to check these judgments by a reading of the whole. When the book was published, requests came to point out passages which would most quickly and clearly indicate the differences between this and the versions it revises. That is a risky procedure. It would be better if every reader would simply read the Revised Standard Version, a book at a time, with the single purpose of getting its message, and only then—after all has been read—form his judgment concerning the relative merits of this and the other versions.

Yet here are some passages that may be used for a quick comparison: Matt. 9.16-17; Matt. 15.1-6; Acts 22, Paul's address to the people of Jerusalem; Acts 24, his defense before

Felix; Acts 27, his shipwreck; Rom. 8; 2 Cor. 5.16-6.13; Phil. 2.1-11; 1 Thess. 4; 2 Tim. 3.14-17; Tit. 1 and 2.

The author of the excellent article which appeared in *The Times Literary Supplement,* London, May 24, 1947, under the title "American New Testament," selects 1 Cor. 7 for special comment:

The passages in the Epistles which deal with sexual morality are especially striking: by a judicious use of current terms, and by rendering such injunctions as (KJ and ERV) "defraud ye not one the other" by "do not refuse one another," the translators have managed to make 1 Corinthians 7 read like a chapter of sound common sense instead of the cento of out-of-date maxims which so many Christians are apt to think it, largely because our existing versions have done St. Paul far less than justice.

Another passage that has acquired new clarity and interest is 2 Cor. 8 and 9, in which Paul explains why he is sending Titus to help the brethren at Corinth collect the liberal gift which they had promised for the relief of the saints at Jerusalem.

In the past fifty years a wealth of individual translations of the New Testament into modern English has appeared. The most widely used of these are *The Twentieth Century New Testament* (1901), Richard F. Weymouth's *The New Testament in Modern Speech* (1902), James Moffatt's *The New Testament: A New Translation* (1913), and Edgar J. Goodspeed's *The New Testament: An American Translation* (1923). Moffatt and Goodspeed were members of the committee which produced the Revised Standard Version, and it owes much to their experience and skill as translators and to the devotion with which they undertook the revision of the Tyndale-King James tradition, a task quite different from that which they had so well accomplished in their own translations.

In 1941 was published *The New Testament of Our Lord and Savior Jesus Christ. Translated from the Latin Vulgate. A Revision of the Challoner-Rheims Version.* This revision was made by twenty-seven Catholic scholars under the patronage of the Episcopal Committee of the Confraternity of Christian Doctrine. It sustains to the Rhemish version a relation analogous to that which the Revised Standard Version sustains to the King James Version, and the revision has been made along much the same lines. This is made from the Latin Vulgate, but the revisers show that they are fully cognizant of the Greek. It is possible that further revision will be made in due time, in view of the papal encyclical *Divino Afflante Spiritu,* November 30, 1943, which authorizes the translation of the Scriptures from the original Hebrew and Greek. Of individual translations made by Roman Catholic scholars, the best is that made from the Latin Vulgate by Monsignor Ronald A. Knox, English priest and man of letters, which was published in 1944.

The concluding chapter of Theodore Maynard's *The Story of American Catholicism,* entitled "The Corporate Vision," is a forthright statement of the hopes of a layman, poet, and man of letters who is a convert to Roman Catholicism. Among the major grounds for hope he describes the Liturgical Revival which looks toward more intelligent participation by the people in the worship of the Roman Catholic Church. I quote a paragraph which reveals how far the spirit of the Church, as understood by Maynard, is removed from the medieval theory and practice which Wycliffe sought to amend:

The Liturgical Revival has as its main object to make the faithful realize how best to assist at Mass. While it is true that presence at Sunday Mass and a modicum of attention is all that is required for the fulfillment of the Church's precept, and that some can assist at Mass with considerable devotion engaged only in private meditation or in the recitation of the rosary, these—and still less the singing of vernacular hymns—are not the best means of attendance. They do not serve to make us realize fully our active participation in the Mass; they do not allow us to be fully aware that we, like the priest on the altar, have a true priesthood, by virtue of our membership in the Mystical Body obtained at baptism, and that we can and should offer Mass with the priest. Since it is Christ, the High Priest, who is offering up the Mass, through the agency of the priest, the laity should do their utmost to exercise the priesthood that they too possess. This is something that anybody can do and that everybody must do who wishes to enter in to the heart of Catholicism.[1]

Maynard goes on to say that "one of the chief reasons for the neglect of the Liturgy has been the Catholic neglect of the Bible from which it is derived"; and he expresses his conviction that much good is to be expected from the revision of the New Testament published by the Confraternity of of Christian Doctrine and the revision of the Old Testament which is in progress. Maynard was writing two years before the issuance of the Papal Encyclical on the promotion of biblical studies; he could now base his hopes upon that authoritative statement of the attitude of the Roman Catholic Church. In this Encyclical Letter Pope Pius XII enjoins upon the faithful the reading of the Scriptures, encourages the study of the Scriptures in the original languages by the methods of sound textual criticism, and authorizes the translation of the Scriptures directly from the original languages into the language of the people.

[1] Copyright 1941 by The Macmillan Co. Used by permission.

The present crisis in human history needs no portraying in any words of mine—its pressure is upon us all. There is no escape from the ruin that threatens mankind by any methods that fall short of moral and spiritual regeneration. Our lives must be undergirded, our decisions made, and our actions sustained, by commitment to those eternal principles of truth and right, justice and love, which God revealed in Jesus Christ. It is a good providence that has led both Roman Catholics and Protestants, in these recent years, to undertake anew the study of the record of that revelation, and to state it in language that people can understand. We now have the resources for a great revival of interest in the Bible, resources that will awaken new zest for its reading and study, and bring new meaning to its use in public and private worship.

The Revised Standard Version of the Bible will not be fully available for use in public worship until the revision of the Old Testament is completed, and the entire Bible can be published in editions intended for the pulpit and the lectern. In the meantime, however, many ministers are reading the New Testament lessons in the services of the church from the Revised Standard Version; and many have written to express their satisfaction with it. "People do not know the difference," say some, explaining that this means that the language of the new version is so like the King James in basic structure as to seem appropriate to use in public worship. "People tell me that now they really listen to the reading of the New Testament," say others, adding that this is because they can understand it as it is read.

The hope of the committee is that ministers and churches generally, without waiting for the entire Bible, will give to the Revised Standard Version of the New Testament an extended period of use in public reading in the church service, as well as use in class instruction and in private reading. Let the experiment be for a year, or at least six months; it is likely that in most cases the new version will continue to be read.

As chairman of the committee, I would be glad to receive criticisms and suggestions arising out of such use of the Revised Standard Version of the New Testament. There will be opportunity, when the work upon the Old Testament is completed and the Bible is to be published as a whole, to consider such criticisms. Some have already been offered that warrant consideration at that time. One is with respect to Paul's quotation from Epimenides (Acts 17.28) which reads in KJ: "In him we live, and move, and have our being." In RSV this reads: "In him we live and move and are." One minister criticizes this sharply, after reading the passage in public worship, on the ground that the word "are" is so commonly a linking verb that the reader is unprepared for the use here made of it, and expects a predicate noun or adjective to follow. Another minister criticizes, "Blessed be he who comes in the name of the Lord" on the ground of euphony, holding that the reading, "Blessed is he . . ." is as well justified by the Greek, and is easier to read. I cite these simply as examples of the kind of criticism and suggestion that may emerge from actual use of the version in public worship.

There are some who advocate the use of two versions, the King James for reading in public worship in the church, and the Revised for private reading, study and teaching. This is not a satisfactory solution of the problem, and as a policy it is unsound in principle. Thought and worship are not incompatible. Jesus' commandment to love God includes the phrase, "with all your mind." Whatever considerations of truth call for the use of the Revised Version in study and teaching call also for its use in public worship.

I have not made any attempt to present the evidence which is decisive against the continued use of the unrevised King James Version. That evidence is drawn from the study of the Greek text, and from our present knowledge of Greek usage. I have dealt only with problems arising in the field of English usage, and have been concerned with the archaisms, obscurities, and infelicities of the King James Version rather than with its actual errors in basic text and translation.

These errors are many, and any one of the Revised Versions of 1881, 1901, and 1946 is unquestionably more correct than the King James Version. I assume that most of us will agree with Professor C. J. Cadoux, who says:

That really ought to settle the question as to which of the two Christians ought consistently to use. Give what weight you please to the arguments about rhythm, music, dignity, and the devotional value arising from long familiarity and sacred associations; these surely ought not, in the judgment of any educated and responsible Christian, to outweigh considerations of truth and falsehood.

To adopt the policy of using the unrevised King James Version in public worship and a revised version for education and evangelism, would be hurtful to both. It would be to make tacit assumption that truth and understanding are of little consequence in worship, and that the feeling of reverence is best elicited by archaic and obscure language. It would be to prevent the newer version from acquiring those associations in worship which are indispensable to its full meaning for the lives of those who read it. It would be to separate pulpit and pew, worship and life, church and education, yet farther, when these are already too far apart.

The adoption of such a policy, finally, would be to turn our backs upon one of the basic principles of the Protestant Reformation—the principle that the Word of God is to be made plain to the people in their own language, and that the reading and exposition of the Word is of central significance in the public worship of God. It was for this principle that Tyndale lived and toiled and suffered martyrdom; and for this his successors labored throughout the sixteenth century, until finally the King James Version was produced. All through that century there were many who took the position that Latin must remain the language of public worship and the English versions be kept for less exalted use. But in the end the truer principle prevailed, and the English Bible moved the minds and hearts of men in public worship as well as in private reading and devotion.

The language of the King James Version is not as strange to the general run of people today as Latin was to the common people of the sixteenth century. But it is strange; and it covers errors which have made revision imperative. The same principle that called forth the translations in the Tyndale-King James series, and that led to their use in the public worship of the church, calls today for the use in public worship of a revised version in this same tradition.

I hope that what I have said may not be taken as lack of appreciation of the King James Version. It is, as John Livingston Lowes has said, "the noblest monument of English prose." It has entered as no other book into the making of the personal character and the public institutions of the English-speaking people. We owe to it an utterly incalculable debt.

The King James translators, were they alive today, would be among the first to recognize the need of revision of their work. The committee which has been charged by the American churches to make that revision has sought to make it in their spirit. Our years of working together have deepened our sense of the significance and urgent importance of the task. It is our hope and our earnest prayer that we may not have failed, but that the Revised Standard Version of the Bible may be used by God to speak to men in these momentous times, and to help them to understand and believe and obey his Word.

Bibliographical Note

THE most helpful books on the general subject of the English New Testament are the two-volume work by John Eadie, *The English Bible* (1876); Philip Schaff, *A Companion to the Greek New Testament and the English Version* (1883; second edition, 1896); T. Lewis O. Davies, *Bible English* (1875); Andrew Edgar, *The Bibles of England* (1889); and Charles C. Butterworth, *The Literary Lineage of the King James Bible* (Philadelphia: Univ. of Pa. Press, 1941). Of other historical accounts the best are Brooke Foss Westcott, *A General View of the History of the English Bible* (London & Cambridge: The MacMillan Co., 1868; third edition revised by W. A. Wright, New York: The Macmillan Co., 1927); Alfred W. Pollard, *Records of the English Bible*, 1911, which reprints sixty-three documents dating from 1525 to 1611; and the volume of essays edited by H. Wheeler Robinson, *The Bible in its Ancient and English Versions* (London: Oxford Univ. Press, 1940). The story of the Greek text and its transmission is told in an interesting popular book by Sir Frederic Kenyon, *The Story of the Bible* (London, John Murray Co., 1936; New York: E. P. Dutton & Sons, 1937).

A book that cannot be too highly praised is Margaret Deanesley, *The Lollard Bible and other Medieval Biblical Versions* (Cambridge: Univ. Press, 1920; New York: The Macmillan Co., 1920), to which I owe some of the quotations in the early part of Chapter II. Two other studies that it is a delight to read are the compact, meaty little books by Bernard L. Manning, *The People's Faith in the Time of Wyclif* (New York: The Macmillan Co., 1919), and by R. R. Williams, *Religion and the English Ver-*

nacular (London: The Sheldon Press, 1940), the latter of which deals particularly with the years 1526 to 1553.

The best work on Tyndale's life was for some years Robert Demaus, *William Tindale, a Biography,* (1871, revised 1886, reprinted 1927); but now we have an even better study of his life and work in J. F. Mozley, *William Tyndale* (London: The Sheldon Press, 1937; New York: The Macmillan Co., 1937).

The most convenient method of comparing the early English versions of the New Testament is to consult *The English Hexapla,* published by Samuel Bagster and Sons in 1841, which is to be found in most college and university libraries. Unfortunately, it does not include the Bishops' Bible. J. G. Carleton's study, *The Part of Rheims in the Making of the English Bible* (London: Oxford Univ. Press, 1902) is valuable.

In 1873 there was published in New York, edited by Philip Schaff, a volume entitled *The Revision of the English Version of the New Testament,* by J. B. Lightfoot, R. V. Trench, and C. J. Ellicott. It reprints and brings together three essays, one by each of these scholars, on the need for revision of the King James Version. These essays remain among the best on the subject, and will amply repay the reader.

The principles which have been followed in the preparation of the Revised Standard Version of the New Testament, published in 1946, are set forth in a pamphlet of seventy-two pages entitled *An Introduction to the Revised Standard Version of the New Testament.* (New York: Thomas Nelson & Sons, 1946.)

This note contains only such titles as I recommend to the general reader who may wish to explore further the subject of this book. I do not attempt to list the sources which I have consulted in its preparation. Some of them are indicated in the text; to name them all would extend this note unduly.

Words With Changed Meanings

∘∘∘

THE following are some of the words in the King James Version of the New Testament that are likely to be misleading because of changes in their meaning. Only one reference is given for each word; others may readily be found in a concordance. The list is by no means complete; it is meant simply to help the reader who may wish to explore the subject further. It does not attempt to list expressions that are archaic or obsolete, but not misleading (such as "an hungred," "go a fishing," "thereabout"). Neither does it list prepositions used in archaic senses (such as "of" and "by") or redundancies (such as "because that," "after that," "but and if").

addicted, 1 Cor. 16.15
admiration, Rev. 17.6
admire, 2 Thess. 1.10
adventure, Acts 19.31
affectioned, Rom. 12.10
afore, Eph. 3.3
aforehand, Mark 14.8
aforetime, John 9.13
albeit, Philem. 19
all manner, Rev. 18.12
allege, Acts 17.3
allow, Luke 11.48
alway, Phil. 4.4
amaze, Mark 14.33

amazement, 1 Pet. 3.6
ambassage, Luke 14.32
anon, Matt. 13.20
barbarian, Rom. 1.14
barbarous, Acts 28.2
base, 2 Cor. 10.1
because, Matt. 20.31
bestow, Luke 12.17
bottle, Matt. 9.17
bowels, Phil. 1.8
broided, 1 Tim. 2.9
by and by, Mark 6.25
canker, 2 Tim. 2.17
cankered, James 5.3

careful, Luke 10.41
carefully, Phil. 2.28
carefulness, 1 Cor. 7.32
carriage, Acts 21.15
chambering, Rom. 13.13
charge, 1 Tim. 5.7
chargeable, 1 Thess. 2.9
charger, Matt. 14.8
coasts, Matt. 2.16
comfort, Acts 16.40
commune, Acts 24.26
communicate, Heb. 13.16
communication, 1 Cor. 15.33
compass, Acts 28.13
comprehend, John 1.5
conclude, Rom. 11.32
concupiscence, Rom. 7.8
conscience, 1 Cor. 8.7
consent, Rom. 7.16
constantly, Acts 12.15
convenient, Eph. 5.4
conversation, 1 Pet. 3.1, 2
convince, John 8.46
covet, 1 Cor. 14.39
creature, Rom. 8.19-21
cumber, Luke 10.40
curious, Acts 19.19
damn, Rom. 14.23
damnable, 2 Pet. 2.1
damnation, 1 Cor. 11.29
debate, Rom. 1.29
degree, 1 Tim. 3.13
delicacy, Rev. 18.3
delicately, Luke 7.25

deliciously, Rev. 18.7, 9
demand, Luke 3.14
deputy, Acts 13.7
despiteful, Rom. 1.30
despitefully, Acts 14.5
doctor, Luke 2.46
doctrine, Mark 4.2
doubt, Acts 5.24
doubtful, Rom. 14.1
dure, Matt. 13.21
either, James 3.12
emulation, Gal. 5.20
endeavor Eph. 4.3
ensample, Phil. 3.17
ensue, 1 Pet. 3.11
entreat, Acts 27.3
estate, Acts 22.5
estate, Col. 4.8
fain, Luke 15.16
fan, Matt. 3.12
feebleminded, 1 Thess. 5.14
fetch, Acts 28.13
for to, Luke 4.16
forwardness, 2 Cor. 9.2
frankly, Luke 7.42
froward, 1 Pet. 2.18
gazingstock, Heb. 10.33
generation, Luke 3.7
ghost, Matt. 27.50
good, 1 John 3.17
grudge, James 5.9
halt, John 5.3
haply, Luke 14.29
hardly, Acts 27.8

harp, 1 Cor. 14.7
heady, 2 Tim. 3.4
heavy, Matt. 26.37
highminded, 1 Tim. 6.17
hoise, Acts 27.40
honest, Phil. 4.8
howbeit, John 6.23
instant, 2 Tim. 4.2
instantly, Acts 26.7
jangling, 1 Tim. 1.6
kindreds, Acts 3.25
latchet, Mark. 1.7
left, Luke 5.4
let, Rom. 1.13
libertines, Acts 6.9
list, Matt. 17.12
lively, 1 Pet. 2.4, 5
mansion, John 14.2
meat, Matt. 6.25
minding, Acts 20.13
naughtiness, James 1.21
needs, Mark 13.7
nephew, 1 Tim. 5.4
occupy, Luke 19.13
often, 1 Tim. 5.23
on sleep, Acts 13.36
overcharge, 2 Cor. 2.5
person, Acts 10.34
persuade, Acts 19.8
piety, 1 Tim. 5.4
presently, Matt. 26.53
prevent, 1 Thess. 4.15
proper, Heb. 11.23
provoke, 2 Cor. 9.2

publican, Luke 3.12
purchase, 1 Tim. 3.13
quarrel, Col. 3.13
quick, Heb. 4.12
reckon, Rom. 8.18
record, Phil. 1.8
rehearse, Acts 11.4
reins, Rev. 2.23
resemble, Luke 13.18
riot, 2 Pet. 2.13
rioting, Rom. 13.13
room, Luke 14.7
scrip, Matt. 10.10
secure, Matt. 28.14
secondarily, 1 Cor. 12.28
seed, John 8.33
set to, John 3.33
shambles, 1 Cor. 10.25
shamefastness, 1 Tim. 2.9
shamefacedness, 1 Tim 2.9
shipmen, Acts 27.30
simple, Rom. 16.19
simplicity, Rom. 12.8
sincerity, Eph. 6.24
sleight, Eph. 4.14
sop, John 13.26
space, Acts 20.31
stanch, Luke 8.44
straw, Matt. 25.24
study, 2 Tim. 2.15
suddenly, 1 Tim. 5.22
suffer, Mark 11.16
tabernacle, Matt. 17.4
table, Luke 1.63

thank, Luke 6.32
thought, Matt. 6.34
throughly, Luke 3.17
translate, Heb. 11.5
trow, Luke 17.9
unspeakable, 2 Cor. 9.15
usury, Matt. 25.27
vile, Phil. 3.21
virtue, Mark 5.30
ware, Acts 14.6

wealth, 1 Cor. 10.24
whiles, Matt. 5.25
whisperers, Rom. 1.29
whisperings, 2 Cor. 12.20
wist, Mark 9.6
wit, 2 Cor. 8.1
without, 2 Cor. 10.13
worship, Luke 14.10
worthy, Luke 12.48
wot, Acts 3.17

Index of Scripture References

oooooooooooooooooooooooooooooooooooooooooooooooo

INDEX OF SCRIPTURE REFERENCES

Index of Names and Subjects